MW00932437

THE LED

Grow Book

Better.
Easier.
Less Watts.

Christopher Sloper

Edited by Laurie Lamberth
Images by Laurie Lamberth

Copyright © 2013 Christopher Sloper.
All rights reserved.

ISBN-10: 1482697327
EAN-13: 978-1482697322

All material within the LED Grow Books is subject to copyright.
No reproduction, electronic storage or transmission of the whole, or any
part, is allowed without the express written permission of the author.

Acknowledgements

To Hai: Thanks...for everything.

To Sheldon: Remember Florida - do you believe me know?

To Stevie "V": Can you believe what you started...two stores and now a book...

To Laurie: Thanks you so much for all your help. This book wouldn't have been nearly as good without you.

Table of Contents

Introduction

I love LED grow lights. I may be the first person you've heard this from, but I won't be the last. The main reason I can't stop preaching about LED grow lights is because they gave me my life back, more or less. That may sound strange, but it's true.

When I used to grow with high-intensity discharge (HID) grow lights, I was consistently worried about the weather. If it was going to be hot, I'd have to make preparations such as leaving the room that supplies intake air to the garden open at night to seriously drop the temperature. Since this room was my bedroom, it was sometimes less than fun it to have it cooled way down. Blankets in summer—weird. I had to run my lights from night into early morning to keep garden temps under control, which meant I had to listen to ventilation fans all night. Plus it was challenging to maintain a garden and have a job when all the garden work needed to be done late at night or early in the morning. It's a lot more stress than anyone should have to endure to produce a successful indoor harvest. I started to hate summer. Then LED grow lights came along. Things got better.

The second reason for loving LED grow lights is the quality of the harvest they produce. In my opinion, LED-grown crops are *significantly* better than crops grown with any other light source I have tried. The amount of terpenes, compounds in a plant responsible for flavor and fragrance, and trichomes, structures that fend off bug attacks, are dramatically higher with LEDs—greater than anything grown under an HID light, including my favorite HID, the ceramic metal halide lamp.

Why This Book?

Before writing this book, I spent lots of time discussing LED grow lights and their benefits with gardeners and grow light manufacturers. Most of these conversations started the same: The person I was talking with had heard that LED grow lights are great for cloning and vegetative growth but not for flowering plants. When I asked if they have had tried LED grow lights personally or were just repeating what others had told them, almost every time it turned out they were just repeating rumors. This is one of the largest problems with LED grow lights—getting past the myths. My goal is to dispel the rumors and teach indoor gardeners how to use LED grow lights properly, so they can produce extraordinary harvests.

I also realized during these conversations that even if someone developed the über, ultimate, perfect LED grow light (you know the one: it uses 1 watt and outgrows the sun!), most gardeners would have no idea what to do with it. Gardeners who currently grow with HID grow lights want to use LED grow lights just like their HIDs, without changing their gardening techniques. Others experiment, making incorrect changes based on existing, incorrect myths. Either way, these growers' results suffer because they don't understand how to successfully garden with LED grow lights, and so their opinions of LED grow lights suffer as well. This book will arm you to make good LED gardening decisions and grow your best garden, even if it's your first.

I truly believe that LED grow lights put quality indoor gardening within everyone's reach. There is no reason that anyone can't grow their own food and herbs at home with ease under LED grow lights. They are so simple compared to HID grow lights: just hang them up and plug them into a timer then into an ordinary wall socket. HID lighting setups, in contrast, often intimidate or confuse inexperienced gardeners. I can't say how many times I watched a new indoor gardener go cross eyed in my hydroponics store when I explained how HID grow lights work.

Some customers would chicken out when they saw the ballast, hood, and lamps. Setting up a multi-part grow light system, which can present a fire hazard if poorly installed, can be too much for someone who just wants to grow their own at home. Other customers bought fluorescent grow lights, since the lights looked like something they were familiar with, but ended up unhappy with their results. A lot of people don't want to put in the time and effort needed to develop the skills necessary to grow with HID lights, which include developing constant vigilance and gardening finesse. Sure, HIDs can produce large yields and be fun for those who are willing to put up with the overhead. LED grow lights make most of that hassle go away.

This book teaches a back-to-basics approach to indoor gardening empowered by LED grow lights. I talk about new good gardening techniques and reinforce some old ones without promoting expensive nutrients and equipment. You really don't need most of the stuff that's sold at your local hydroponics shop. Sure, some of it works well, but a lot of it is "snake oil" promising massive increases in yields that are rarely realized in actual harvests. Some "cutting edge" products can actually harm your yields unless they are applied *exactly* right. Here, you'll learn how to make indoor gardening simple and less expensive so that everyone can grow their own at home with LEDs.

I also encourage indoor gardeners to consider more energy-efficient alternatives to *every* watt they use in their gardens. A lot has changed since decades ago when the indoor gardening community began using HID grow lights to cultivate indoor gardens. Before then, HIDs were only used for lighting factories, streets and stadiums. It's time to evolve new "common" gardening techniques that use less electricity. We will discuss these opportunities in great detail; by the time you're done reading this book, you'll be on your way to bigger, better harvests that take less energy—both electrical and human—to grow.

Who Should Read This Book?

This book is targeted to indoor growers who would otherwise use a single 250 watt HID up to two 600-watt HID grow lights. While gardening indoors is a fantastic hobby, many people have tried and failed or believe they have a "black thumb" based on other gardening experiences. LED grow lights ease the strain with simple lighting setup and simplified environmental controls. They allow people to learn to grow indoors without having to become either an engineer or a slave to their gardens.

This book is specifically *not* targeted to the multi-1000-watt light commercial grower, due to the high initial cost and rapid development path of LED grow lights. It may be hard for commercial growers to recoup their investments before wanting to upgrade to newer LED grow lights. The best path for commercial growers is to begin experimenting with LED grow lights in a small part of their gardens to gain experience and be ready when LED grow light prices and features balance at a point more practical for commercially scaled gardens.

In the meantime, for you personal growers, if you're ready to grow easily for yourself, read on.

How This Book Is Organized

In the first half of this book, you will learn about LEDs and the grow lights that use them. After that, we'll walk through the main gardening topics that all indoor gardeners have to wrestle with in their quest to become "Mom Nature": managing your garden in harmony with plant growth phases, designing an effective grow space, choosing a grow system, feeding your plants, and dealing with pests. You'll learn how LED grow lights affect the process of managing your garden, and how easy LED gardening can be compared to the alternatives.

As you read this book, you'll come across tips for better gardening, enclosed in boxes by category:

 Sloper Says

Insights gained from my personal gardening experience.

 Gardening Zen

Making gardening easier and more peaceful.

 Safety First!

Things that could be dangerous to plants or people.

 Good Practice

Gardening practices that help you grow heavy, high-quality harvests.

 Expert Corner

In-depth material for those who'd like to learn more.

 Fun Fact

Funny or unexpected information about gardening.

1: Why LED Grow Lights Now?

A common question about LED grow lights is "Are they ready for prime time?" That's an easy question to answer: YES, because they have been for a while and they are just getting better and better. Many developments and trends make LED grow lights the right choice for indoor gardeners, now. These include improved emitters, secondary optics, increasing electric rates, reduced waste, and ease of use.

Better Emitters

One of the biggest factors limiting the market potential for LED grow lights until recently was the availability of LED emitters that produce the correct spectra of light needed for needed for photosynthesis, particularly 660-nanometer (nm) emitters. "Nanometers" measure the energy in light and describe how big (how small, actually) the wavelength of light is at various points along the light spectrum. The 660nm emitter emits light in the far end of the red spectrum and is particularly important for photosynthesis.

It's amusing to see how many LED grow light manufacturers claim to be the first or only manufacturer to use "true 660nm emitters." Before 660nm emitters were manufactured, LED grow lights definitely lacked the power and punch needed for good harvests. Now, a few years later, more powerful emitters in a wider range of colors have spawned a new generation of LED grow lights. These newer LED lights offer significantly improved spectrum and output strength compared to earlier generations.

Secondary Optics

A second, huge area of improvement is the "secondary optics" being paired with LED emitters. These small plastic focusing lenses are positioned atop LED emitters to intensify the light and direct it downward and outward. Secondary optic lenses significantly improve the evenness of the light over the plants' canopy and penetration deep into the plants. There is lots of research going into secondary optics, so expect to see more innovation here in the future.

Increasing Electrical Rates

Higher electrical rates provide significant incentives to switch to LED grow lights now. In Southern California, our electrical provider SoCal Edison (SCE) has announced that electrical rates will rise every year for the next few years. A 1000-watt high-intensity discharge (HID) light running a 12-hour bloom cycle every day uses 4.3 megawatts of electricity in a year. At SCE's current peak rate of $0.36 per kilowatt-hour, it costs more than $1,500 per year to run one 1000-watt grow light, and that does not include the electricity to maintain the environment, such as air conditioning and ventilation fans. LED grow lights can cut that expenditure in half or more.

Possibly aggravating this problem, electric utilities across the United States and around the world are rolling out digital electric meters known as "smart meters." These new meters are more accurate at measuring electricity than their magnetic forebears. There are reports of electric consumers who ended up paying 10% more—or worse—after their smart meter was installed. These customers were not being overcharged because of

Electrical Rates are Going Through the Roof!

their new electric meter. Instead they were actually (finally) being charged the correct amount for the electricity they used.

And while this would certainly never apply to anyone reading this book, a word of warning to the unscrupulous growers out there who've been stealing electricity to power their grow: you won't be able to get away with it going forward. Behind smart meters is the "smart grid," consisting of today's electric grid overlaid with a two-way communication network and high-tech tools to manage the flow of electricity and improve efficiency. This network allows utilities to track each kilowatt from their generators to the outlets in your home and gives them new tools to catch electrical thieves. Old tricks like bypassing the meter or using magnets to slow or reverse it won't work anymore. You may be facing felony grand theft charges if you continue.

Reduction in Hazardous Waste

Another reason to switch to LED grow lights is that they generate less waste. Commercial indoor gardeners replace their HID lamps as often as every six months, hobbyists generally once a year. Some of these spent lamps contain mercury and must be disposed of as toxic waste, but unfortunately many of them end up in the trash—adding heavy metals to our landfills that can leach into the water supply. This toxic waste stream is completely eliminated with LED grow lights, though the grow lights themselves must be disposed of as "e-waste" (similar to computers) at the end or their useful lives.

While some HID lamp manufacturers have removed the mercury from their bulbs, many of the cheap lamps still contain it. Besides the disposal issue, these lamps may also generate a bigger toxic waste problem: heavy metals on your crop. Some lighting experts recommend strongly against using mercury-containing lamps, because their research shows that these lamps can "spray" vaporized mercury out of the lamp and onto the garden, coating your crops. While not all gardening experts agree with this controversial finding, why take the chance that your grow light could poison your crop?

Ease of Use

Yet another reason for why "now" for LEDs is their consumer-friendly form factor. They are so easy to use: just hang them up and plug them into a timer. There's no separate ballast to hook up or air ducting to connect, adjust, or worse fall off. There are no lamps to change when switching from vegetative to bloom stages, ever. Also gone are potentially hazardous situations that can arise when handling HID lamps: no burns from hot lamps, no chance to drop the lamp into your garden and damage either your plants or the lamp, and no worries about the lamp potentially exploding from contaminates not removed after handling or nutrient solution splashed up during watering or spraying.

What's Wrong with HID Garden Lights?

HID grow lights, whether high-pressure sodium (HPS), metal halide (MH), or ceramic metal halide (CMH), all are effective at growing plants indoors when properly used. While each type has its pluses and minuses, HIDs have dominated the indoor garden market for decades despite their limitations—heat being the primary enemy.

HIDs produce lots of photons (a single packet of light energy at a specific wavelength) that can easily penetrate deep into a garden's canopy. Using HPS and MH lamps in combination, or switching between MH and HPS for vegetative and flowering stages, has worked for indoor gardeners for a long time. Why change?

 **Expert Corner**

In this book, high-pressure sodium (HPS), metal halide (MH), and ceramic metal halide (CMH) are referred to as "HID grow lights" or HIDs. They are similar and often don't need to be distinguished from each other. All of them create unnecessary heat and deliver a single, manufacturer-determined light spectrum.

"The Most Un-Green Thing in Our Gardens"

The first blow against HIDs is that they produce too much heat for the amount of light they generate. A 1000-watt HPS lamp is only about 40% efficient when it comes to growing plants: it produces approximately 400 watts of "photosynthetically active radiation" (PAR) between 400nm and 700nm, plus 600 watts of "heat" energy above 700nm. This heat comes from the method used to create the light. HID lamps superheat a mixture of mineral salts until they glow.

The waste heat produced from these hot salt mixtures must go somewhere. Unless removed, it will go straight into your garden's canopy—raising temperatures, speeding up transpiration, and eventually drying out both the plants and their growing media. Waste heat is expensive to produce and even more expensive to remove. Both sides of that equation needlessly burn electricity.

Wasted versus Targeted Spectrum

Equally troublesome, most HIDs were designed to help humans see, not so that plants could grow under them. Their light spectrum is not optimal for photosynthesis: much of the light they emit is in the middle of the visible spectrum, where human eyesight is optimized but photosynthesis is not. HID lamp manufacturers have been able to tweak their lamp chemistries a little bit to create HID lamps with a more desirable spectrum for plants, such as the "blue enhanced" HPS lamps sold in hydroponics shops. Still these lamps produce more heat than usable light.

HID lamp manufacturers can only go so far to improve their PAR ratings without making major changes from the ground up, at great expense and with limited gain in performance. Not only are the possible improvements in HID lamp suitability for photosynthesis limited by technology, the indoor gardening market is tiny compared to the general lighting market. Research-and-development budgets for HID grow lights are small compared to those for street, parking lot, and stadium lights, so radical innovation is unlikely to emerge.

Why Haven't LED Lights Taken Over the Market?

Even with their advantages, several factors have been holding LED grow lights back. While the primary reason for slow adoption is their high upfront cost, hype from LED grow light manufacturers, bad results from early adopters, and a general lack of knowledge of how to garden effectively with LED grow lights have all taken their toll. Market forces, particularly economies of scale, also stand in the way.

LED Emitters Haven't Hit Scale

The main reason LED grow lights cost so much is the cost of the LEDs themselves, normally called LED "emitters" or "chips." LED manufacturing is analogous to computer chip manufacturing. Remember how expensive personal computers were when they were first introduced? That's because the chips were expensive to manufacture. Back in the 1980s, chip manufacturers expected to yield one or two good chips out of two dozen or more on an individual round "platter." Flashing forward to today, if one or two chips failed on a platter, the manufacturer would stop the production line to figure out what was wrong. Improvements in manufacturing technology have driven the cost of computer chips significantly down, which in turn reduces the cost of the whole computer and allows retail prices to fall.

The manufacturing process for LED emitters is expensive, and it produces a wide range of emitter quality levels from batch to batch. Like early computer chips, only a small number of LED emitters produced using current processes are top quality. The rest are used for lower-quality grow lights and traffic signals. The good news for us indoor gardeners is that the price of LED emitters decreases almost daily. Globally, tons of money is being spent on LED research that is driving better, more cost-efficient manufacturing and lower costs for higher-quality emitters.

There's a new announcement just about every week about LED advances, it seems, and demand for LED lights of all types is skyrocketing. Just look around: suddenly every light source is changing to LEDs. From traffic control lights to streetlights, stadium lights, cop cars, and holiday lights, LEDs are spreading like wildfire. Growing demand for LEDs gives LED manufacturers serious incentives to reduce costs and capture a growing share of this market. Indoor gardeners will benefit from this rising tide, with respect to both LED grow light cost and quality.

Early Adopter Problems

The "early adopters" are also very much to blame in hindering the spread of LED grow lights, even though this was opposite their intent. Many early adopters, some of whom built their own LED grow lights, posted the results of their experiments online. With a few notable exceptions, online pictures of early LED grows were quite unappealing: poor-quality photos of scraggly plants that chilled grower interest in LED grow lights. It seems these growers fell into the trap of believing that hanging a new light would improve their garden, instead of focusing on improving their gardening skills.

Looking at some of these results could convince a reasonable person that LEDs don't work or are still a long way off. Keep in mind that only a small number of gardeners post pictures of their gardens online. Don't believe these results, and don't get scared away. There are a lot of very successful LED gardens, hopefully soon to including yours—but nobody gets to see them.

Education

The biggest reason LED grow lights aren't used more is the lack of this book! No educational materials currently exist to help gardeners understand how to adjust their gardening style to work with LED grow lights. This book gives you a framework for selecting the proper LED grow light for the type of growing you want to do, plus techniques that will help you succeed. LED grow lights are wonderful indoor garden tools, and some day they may hang in every indoor garden. This book will help you unlock the mysteries, challenge the myths, and make LED grow lights work for you.

One the most difficult concepts to get across to indoor gardeners is that any time you make one change in your garden, you will have to make other changes as well. Your garden is a living ecosystem: one change can upset the status quo and lead to other changes. A "change" includes switching to a different growing media, changing nutrients, buying a new light, or changing a ventilation fan.

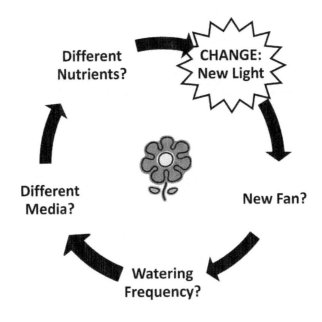

One Garden Change Can Lead to Others

Switching to an LED grow light is a major garden change, yet many gardeners don't recognize it as such. The "simple" action of replacing an HID grow light with a LED grow light prompts the need to reexamine everything about garden setup and practice. If you're currently gardening with HIDs, the methods you're currently using in your garden may not work with LED grow lights.

For example, a LED grow light produces less heat: do you need a different fan? Cooler temps will reduce the level of evaporation: do you need to revise your watering schedule or switch to a growing media that retains less moisture? Plants transpire more slowly in lower temperatures: is your nutrient solution too strong? Did your humidity go up or down as a result these changes? If so, you may need to think more creatively about ventilation.

Now is the time to open your eyes and tune into your plants. They will tell you everything you need to know if you are able to understand them. Even if you're an experienced gardener, when you switch to LED grow lights, think of yourself as a rookie grower again, and pay close attention to how your actions affect your garden. Over a few harvests, you'll develop you own technique and soon be overgrowing the planet. You can't learn everything you need to know from a single grow. This is normal and to be expected.

2: Myths about Grow Lights

Most likely it's the many myths, some started by the light manufacturers themselves, which have given LED grow lights such a bad reputation with indoor gardeners. It seems as if many LED lighting manufacturers don't actually grow with their lights: their leadership team usually consists of a lighting engineer, plus an entrepreneur with an interest in gardening. Neither of them has much indoor gardening experience, if any. They're chasing the next trend with the hope of turning a dollar, and with little practical gardening experience backing up their claims, they have inadvertently poisoned their market with misinformation.

To be fair, it's not all of the LED guys, and it's not just them. The indoor gardening industry itself has perpetuated these myths out of ignorance. It's easy to believe "facts" about LED grow lights when the same message comes from multiple trustworthy sources, including the distributors and magazines that serve the hydroponics industry.

What do you say we bust some of these myths?

Myth 1: Lumens = Photosynthesis

Silly grower…lumens are for humans! That lumens are an appropriate way to measure light produced by a grow light is the all-time number-one indoor gardening myth. Measuring light intended for photosynthesis in lumens is just plain stupid. Let's be clear: a lumen (scientific symbol: lm) is a measurement of how much light the human eye perceives. It does not, in any way, measure the light that drives photosynthesis. Period. Simply put, lumens measure the total amount of human visible light that comes from a particular light source.

Plants and humans evolved under the same light, coming from the sun. But humans and plants use this light very differently. Humans use most of the "visible light range" between 400nm and 700nm, but our eyes are focused on 500–600nm, mostly the green and yellow portions of the spectrum. Plants have a completely different response to light, focusing their absorption around 400nm–500nm (blue) and 600nm–700nm (red). They also absorb some light in the rest of the visible spectrum as well as non-visible light in the ultraviolet and infrared bands.

 Expert Corner

It's difficult to understand the "lumens versus micromoles" topic if you're not a physicist. Light science is very complex, and the explanations provided here are highly distilled for a nonscientific audience.

To understand the complexity of light science, one only has to look up "lumen" in Wikipedia, the crowdsourced online encyclopedia. The "Explanation" section begins: "If a light source emits one candela of luminous intensity uniformly across a solid angle of one steradian, the total luminous flux emitted into that angle is one lumen (1 cd·1 sr = 1 lm)."

Apologies to any physicists in the audience who would prefer a more detailed definition. Go ahead, correct me—write your own book!

Measuring grow light output in lumens is an artifact of the lighting industry itself. Since light bulb manufacturers focus mainly on illumination for humans, they publish their lamp specifications in lumens. Some countries require light bulbs to rated according to lumen output. Indoor gardeners have adopted this method for measuring the brightness of their grow lights since it's generally available from the lamp manufacturers (at least up until LEDs came on to the scene).

When it comes to garden lighting, it's time to stop thinking in lumens and start thinking about "photosynthetic photon flux density" (PPFD), which describes the density of photons reaching a particular surface area. PPFD is measured in "micromoles (µmol) per meter^2 per second," which is a more useful measurement for the light your plants receive than lumens. You need a quantum flux meter to measure how much photosynthetically active light energy is actually reaching your plants. When testing LED grow lights, make sure to pick a quantum flux meter that is specifically designed for LEDs, or your measurements will be off. Unfortunately, these devices are very expensive.

Myth 2: Summer-to-Winter Kelvin Shift

A well-respected garden writer recently wrote this in one of the most popular indoor gardening magazines: "The [high-pressure] sodium light is very red and mimics the fall sun to induce flowering." HID lamp salesmen and hydro shop owners also claim that MH lamps are best for vegetative growth because they are "blue" like spring sunlight while HPS lamps are best for flowering because they resemble "red" fall light.

This is the second most widely held gardening myth: that the color of sunlight changes dramatically between seasons and that this color shift induces flowering. Ask yourself this: at midday, does a spring day look blue to you or a fall day look red? In a word, *No.*

Light "color" is measured according to the Kelvin (K) scale with blue having higher values and red lower ones. The world would look very strange indeed if the light temperature of sunlight changed from season to season by anything even close to the 2000–2500K difference between MH and HPS lamps. Don't misunderstand: There *is* a seasonal shift in daylight color due to the depth of the atmosphere the sun's light has to penetrate before reaching the earth. But this shift is small, 300–500K depending where you live, which is a difference that's barely perceptible to the human eye.

On the other hand, daylight color definitely shifts across the duration of a single day. Sunlight starts out in the morning at approximately 2000K (orange), climbs above 5000K (white) at midday, then drops back to 2000K or lower at sunset. Daylight-sky color temp can climb as high as 8,000–10,000K (blue) on a sunny summer afternoon.

Why does this matter? Because indoor gardeners have been taught that changing from "spring blue" to "fall red" will induce flowering—in other words, will cause plants to shift from their vegetative growth phase to their flowering phase. This belief is likely the downstream effect of how HID lights found their way into indoor gardens. Initially, only MH lamps were available, and growers using them experienced results that were...OK. Then HPS lamps were introduced, and the gardeners who tried them found that these new lights significantly improved the weight of their harvests. Someone postulated that MH was better for vegetative growth and HPS better for flowering, and the myth was born. It's become a mainstream "fact": pick up any of the magazines distributed in hydroponics shops and you'll find it. That doesn't make it true.

Many gardeners use only one type of HID light for their entire grow, and that includes MH, HPS, and CMH lamps. None of these gardeners has any trouble "flipping" their gardens from vegetative to fruiting/flowering. They simply changed the photoperiod—the length of time the lights are turned on. Plants that are sensitive to day length flower when their photoperiod changes, *not* when the color of the light they receive changes.

Myth 3: 90 LED Watts Can Replace 400–600 HID Watts

Oh, how you missed out on the fun of the early days of LED grow lights! When LED grow lights were first introduced, many manufacturers boldly proclaimed that a single 90-watt LED grow light would out-produce a 400- or 600-watt HID. These claims were laughable then, and they're still laughable now. LED grow light manufacturers have typically been overzealous with their claims, which they "prove" by growing wheatgrass or lettuce instead of the light-hungry crops (e.g., tomatoes, cucumbers, herbs, or flowers) that indoor gardeners generally prefer.

Testing revealed that these early "90-watt" units actually drew only 54–56 watts of power at the wall, on average. With a few watts going to power onboard cooling fans, these lights actually produced less usable light than 75–100 watts of HPS—not anywhere near the 400- or 600-watt HID performance claimed by their manufacturers.

90 LED Grow Light Watts ≠ 400-600 HID Watts

At least the industry seems to have learned its lesson. These days, most LED grow light manufacturers provide realistic power ratings and coverage area recommendations for their lights. This combined with better, more powerful LEDs and more effective light designs are helping to end this myth. It would be ideal for LED grow light manufacturers to publish the power of their lights in micromoles at set height intervals so that we, their customers, could decide for ourselves how much HID these lights could replace in the actual conditions we face in our gardens.

Myth 4: This Could be the Last Grow Light You'll Ever Buy

Because LED emitters have a 50,000-hour-plus life-span, which is about 10 years if used 12 hours a day, a common sales pitch is: "This could be the last grow light you'll buy." This pitch is intended to help the buyer overcome the high cost of an LED grow light. Unfortunately, it just doesn't work that way.

Even though LED emitters have very long useful lives, continuing innovation in light design, such as secondary optics, better heat management, and still-better LED emitters on the horizon, will cause most growers to upgrade to a newer, better-performing light well before they've put 10 years on their first LED grow light. So while "the last light you'll ever buy" makes a great sales pitch, don't believe it. It's not true.

Myth 5: LEDs Produce Little to No Heat

The next-most-common sales pitch for LED grow lights is that they produce little to no heat. When a manufacturer claims that an LED grow light produces almost no heat, it makes the experienced gardener wonder whether the manufacturer has ever used one for anything more than a photo shoot. Sure, LED grow lights produce *less* heat than HID grow lights, but there is still heat, and that heat needs to be managed. See for yourself: garden temperature will drop immediately after an LED grow light switches off, just like in an HID garden. No heat-no way!

Myth 6: LEDs Won't Burn Plants

One of the biggest myths about LED grow lights is that they won't burn plants no matter how close they're positioned to the plants. This myth is based on the light's relatively low heat output and the idea "the more photons the better." Early LED grow lights, with their lower output, could be positioned close to plants—as close as a fluorescent light, in some cases. With today's high-powered units, it's easy to exceed the light-gathering limit for plants.

When hung too close to plants, LED grow lights can cause photooxidation or "light bleaching." This occurs when more light is absorbed than can be processed by the plant. Those portions of the plant that are closest to the light—often the biggest flowers, unfortunately—turn white because their chlorophyll is destroyed. Both LED and HID grow lights can bleach plants when improperly used, though the problem is less common with HIDs because their high heat output will generally cause the gardener to raise the light, eliminating the threat.

Myth 7: Blue Only for Vegetative, Red Only for Flowering

Just after their introduction, some LED companies were pitching *only* blue light for vegetative growth and *only* red light for flowering. There are still a few lights on the market that make this claim. As with the "90 watts = 400/600 watts" myth, this approach *might* work for low-light crops such as wheatgrass, but light-loving plants need a more complete spectrum to grow properly. Don't fall for it.

3: About LED Grow Lights

What is an LED?

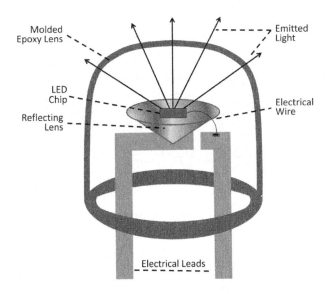

Components of an LED Emitter

LED is an acronym for light emitting diode. LEDs differ from HID lamps in that they use a semiconductor diode to produce light instead of creating light from hot, glowing gas plasma. When an electric current is passed through an LED, a tiny chunk of material at the center of the emitter called a "die" glows a particular color depending on the material it's made from. The die sits in a reflective cup to direct the light outward through an affixed epoxy lens, and then the entire thing is enclosed in an epoxy case.

A grow light made with LEDs consists of the emitters, a heat sink, drivers, cooling fans, and a housing to enclose it all. Individual emitters are connected to the heat sink, which along with cooling fans disperses the heat the LEDs generate. The light's driver, analogous to a ballast in HID lighting, provides power to the emitters. In newer-generation LED grow lights, the emitters are topped with secondary optics to focus and intensify their light.

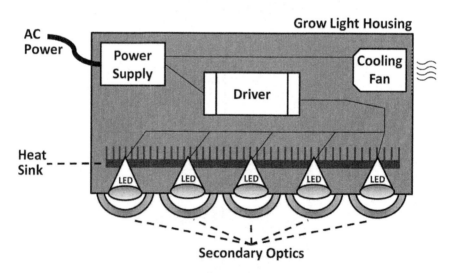

Major Components of an LED Grow Light (not to scale)

What's Different About LED Grow Lights?

LEDs open up a whole new world for indoor gardening. Now we can control the exact wavelengths of light that reach our plants instead of adapting our gardening methods to what's available. We can create plant-specific lights that are efficient for growing a particular crop. The operating characteristics of LED grow lights, particularly the fact that they create less heat, pave the way for smaller gardens tucked into a larger variety of spaces. Here's a run-down of the standout qualities of LED grow lights that you can harness for your indoor garden.

Less Heat

As previously discussed, LED grow lights produce less heat than HIDs. While explaining heat is a rather complicated topic best left for the physics crowd, there are some important things for the rest of us to know. Ask yourself this: What happens when the light is switched off? The photons of light cease to exist, but what happens to them?

Physics tells us that photons "decay" into the "system," which in this case is the grow room. This phenomenon is described in the theory of conservation of energy, which states that energy cannot be created or destroyed—it can only be converted form one form to another. This is a long way of saying that when light decays, it ultimately becomes heat.

By definition, 1 watt of electricity equals 3.412 British Thermal Units (BTU) of heat. This is completely true for all light sources—HID lamp, fluorescent light, LED, or any other light source. It makes no difference.

So why do LEDs produce less heat? It's simple: with LED grow lights, most gardeners use less watts—somewhere between 50% to 60% of HID watts. Less watts equals less heat.

An additional reason LEDs produce less heat is that HID lamps, especially HPS lamps, produce a lot of waste heat in the infrared (IR) region of the light spectrum. IR heats the surfaces it comes in contact with and has been used for decades to heat bathrooms and keep food warm in restaurants. Recently, IR ovens and barbeques have become available. IR energy does nothing but heat up your plants and stress them out.

Expert Corner

Infrared heaters work by heating exposed surfaces, which in turn heat the surrounding air. This is the opposite of traditional heaters where they heat the air then the air warms the surfaces. Keep in mind that in your garden, those surfaces being heated are your plants' leaves and stems!

If lamp manufacturers published spectral power distribution (SPD) charts that went beyond the typical end point of 750nm, it would be easier to understand where this extra IR heat energy comes from. SPD charts that go up to at least 900nm would provide a way to compare some of the heat generated by different light sources. The chart below shows that HPS lights generate large peaks around 810nm-plus, which is all IR heat—quite a lot, in fact, compared to the PAR light emitted.

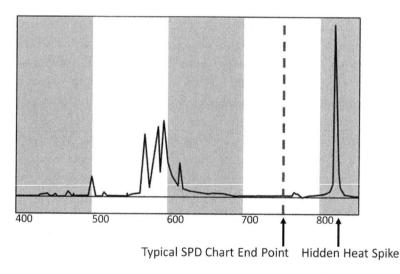

Typical SPD Chart End Point   Hidden Heat Spike

Spectral Distribution (SPD) of a High-Pressure Sodium Light

New Spectra Not Available Under HID

Indoor gardeners will attempt to grow with any lighting technology that comes along. Whether fluorescent, metal halide, high-pressure sodium, low-pressure sodium, ceramic metal halide, induction, LED, or plasma, every new lighting technology will eventually take its turn in an indoor gardening trial. All of these lighting technologies except LEDs have the same problem: you're stuck with the spectrum that manufacturer produces, which is limited by the physical properties of the grow light itself.

One of the best things about LED grow lights is the ability to control the specific light energy your plants receive. Want more blue? If your light allows it, add more blue emitters. If not, supplement with an all-blue LED fixture. If you want more red, add it. Many LED grow light manufacturers will accept special orders for grow lights with custom spectrum colors. If you want to grow with or test a particular spectrum mix in your garden, that's now possible.

"Tunable" Lights

Some LED grow lights offer a "tunable spectrum," which allow all of the reds or blues to be turned up or down together on separate knobs. While some growers don't see much of an advantage to the tunable lights that are on the market today, other growers believe that turning down the reds shortens the internodal distance on plants—the vertical stem height between the flower or leaf sites.

For years, gardening "best practices" have held that internodal distances are best kept short by placing the light at the proper height and not making the plants "reach" for a light that is positioned too high. This holds true for LED grow lights. The risk of depriving your garden of the light it needs by goofing up the settings on tunable LED grow lights exceeds the potential benefit from monkeying with the spectrum.

Down the road, tunable lights will have multiple knobs or settings that control each wavelength independently, allowing the gardener to finely tune his or her light mix. These multi-adjustable lights will help unlock the spectrum secrets of many plants and will likely lead to the development of plant- or strain-specific LED grow lights. Additionally, commercial greenhouse gardeners who rotate different crops through their grow spaces could find plant-specific lights or tunings beneficial, as they could supplement their garden's light with only the spectra necessary for a specific plant.

Total Cost of Ownership: Consider What's Reduced

The initial cost of an LED grow light is significantly higher than for an HID light, by a factor of 3X or more. This higher up-front cost is recovered by way of lower operating costs, notably by lower electrical usage. The cost-recovery time for an LED grow light versus an HID might be shorter than you think. This is because many other products commonly used in indoor gardens can be eliminated or reduced when using an LED grow light compared to an HID-lit garden, lowering electrical consumption even more than the savings from the LED grow light alone.

Cooling Equipment

A major saving with LED gardens is in reduced cooling costs. Traditionally, cooling consumes a large part of total energy used in an indoor garden. Since LED grow lights emit less heat, there is less to remove, leading to savings in both utility bills and equipment costs.

For example, air conditioners may no longer be required. Instead, you may be able to control garden temps using intake and exhaust fans to vent heated air out of the garden and draw cooler outside air in. Not running the A/C can save a lot of energy, plus it's good for the environment since it eliminates the chance of ozone-depleting gasses escaping from a damaged or leaky A/C unit.

Smaller-capacity ventilation fans may be used since there is less heat to remove. If you use a single exhaust fan, don't go too small, as this fan has two jobs: to exchange the air in your garden and remove excess heat. Its size is dependent on the size of your grow space, as well as the heat given off by your grow light. Additional fans used in the garden may be smaller or eliminated entirely, such as inline fans to vent air-cooled hoods and secondary exhaust fans that kick on when garden temps exceed a set threshold. In addition, smaller fans need smaller filters. This is another cost saver since smaller filters are cheaper to buy and replace.

High-Temp Shut Down Controller

One of the most important safety devices in an HID garden is a high-temp shutdown system. This is because the excess heat generated by an HID grow light can fry your garden within a few short hours if the light stays on but ventilation fails.

Since there is less heat produced and accumulated with LED grow lights, the threat of a heat-based garden disaster is significantly reduced, if not eliminated altogether. These devices fall into the "nice to have" category for LED gardens: it's less likely that an LED grow light that continues to operate after the fans shut down could dry out your garden enough to cause a fire, but an unvented HID grow light certainly offers that potential. Growers with large, multi-light LED gardens might want to consider high-temp shutdown controllers to shut down half of the lights if a temp threshold is crossed.

Fire Suppression

As above, the amount of heat generated by HID lamps and ballasts creates a real potential for a fire in your garden should something go seriously wrong. Now that cost effective, automatic fire-suppression products are on the market, they should be deployed in any garden that uses 1000-watt HID lamps, and are a good idea for gardens lit by 400- or 600- watt HIDs.

With LED grow lights, automatic fire-suppression systems are simply not required. It's a good idea to keep a small fire extinguisher nearby "just in case" something else goes awry, but it's a "nice to have" accessory rather than a necessity.

Wall Coverings

Traditionally, indoor gardeners cover grow room walls with reflective material to bounce the unused light back into the garden and thereby maximize the light output of lighting equipment. Since LEDs are highly directional, meaning that their light just goes down onto the plants and doesn't bounce all over the place, it doesn't make sense to spend money on reflective wall coverings in an LED garden. Flat white paint is a lot cheaper than fancy wall films and almost as good from a reflective standpoint. Be sure to use flat paint, not glossy: the glossy part of the paint actually makes it less reflective. White paint also makes it easy to see nutrient splashes or mold infestations that need to be cleaned up at the end of a grow run.

Space Requirements

While it's doesn't generate direct cost savings, one of the more exciting things about LED grow lights is that they allow for plants to be grown in much smaller spaces. Physically smaller lights, smaller fans, less equipment in the grow room—people who could not find a suitable location in their houses for an indoor garden may discover that they can now grow indoors. You no longer need a full-height closet: half of one can easily converted into an LED grow space.

As much as two to three feet in vertical height can be saved in LED gardens from various sources, including these:

- LED lights at 2 to 4 inches thick save 6 to 10 inches in vertical height versus 8 to 14-inch-thick HID reflectors.

- LED grow lights are typically positioned within 6 to 18 inches above the plants, while HID lamps are 18 to 36 inches above plants, saving another 12 to 18 inches.
- There is no need to position intake and exhaust fans above the light to air-cool the reflector. Depending on the setup, this equipment can consume another 6 to 12 vertical inches.
- Secondary ventilation fans, if used, are smaller-sized, as are their filters, saving additional height.

4: LEDs and Photosynthesis

Now it's time to get geeky. Hopefully, you didn't start turning to the next chapter because this information will help you understand how plants and light work together. You need to have a basic understanding of photosynthesis in order to know what to look for in a grow light—any grow light, including an LED.

Stated simply, photosynthesis is the process by which plants convert light energy into the sugars they use as building blocks and energy stores. Membranes in plants called chlorophylls do the heavy lifting, collecting light energy and passing it along to chemical processes inside the leaves that convert light, water, and carbon dioxide (CO_2) from the air into sugars. The reaction looks like this:

Water (H_2O) + light (hv) + Carbon Dioxide (CO_2) → Sugars + Oxygen (O_2)

Photosynthesis can be broken down into two sub-processes: light-dependent reactions and light-independent reactions. It might be simpler to consider the light-dependent reactions "water side" reactions because they use light energy to break up a water molecule (H_2O). The energy produced from these reactions is captured in two compounds that fuel the rest of the photosynthetic process: ATP (adenosine triphosphate) and NADPH (nicotinamide adenine dinucleotide phosphate). Below is the simplified reaction:

$$H_2O + light \rightarrow ATP + NADPH + O_2$$

As with everything in biology, the names can be confusing. "Light-independent reactions" are more commonly called "dark reactions," though they don't only occur at night as their name might imply. They just don't require light, so it's better to call them light-independent reactions.

 **Expert Corner**

Light-independent reactions are also called the "Calvin Cycle." Melvin Calvin, James Bassham, and Andrew Benson discovered it while working together at University of California, Berkeley, but Calvin gets the name recognition.

In these reactions, CO_2 is converted into sugars with the aid of the energy building blocks produced by the light-dependent reactions, ATP and NADPH. Because these reactions consume CO_2, they can be considered "carbon fixation" reactions. Simplified, the carbon fixation reaction looks like this:

$$ATP + NADPH + CO_2 \rightarrow Sugars + O_2$$

Both halves put together:

Light-Dependent Cycle $H_2O + light \rightarrow$ $ATP + NADPH + O_2$
Light-Independent Cycle $\underline{ATP + NADPH + CO_2 \rightarrow Sugars}$
Total Two-Step Reaction $H_2O + light \rightarrow$ $ATP + NADPH + CO_2$
   $\rightarrow Sugars + O_2$

Chlorophyll

Chlorophyll is probably the best-known plant pigment. It's green in color and found in all plants and algae. Chlorophyll's job is to absorb energy from the light photons to which the plant is exposed. In plants, chlorophylls absorb in the red and blue regions of visible light. This may be why early LED manufacturers, who didn't know better, produced grow lights with only red and blue emitters.

One curiosity about chlorophyll is its close resemblance to hemoglobin, the human molecule that provides oxygen and carbon dioxide transport throughout the body. The primary difference between chlorophyll and hemoglobin is their center ion: hemoglobin has iron (Fe) at its center, while chlorophyll centers on magnesium (Mg); otherwise, the molecules are strikingly similar.

 Fun Fact

Did you know there are several types of chlorophyll? Most green plants use chlorophyll A and chlorophyll B plus compounds called caretines to capture light for photosynthesis. There are also C1, C2, D, and F chlorophylls, but these are generally found in lower plant forms such as algae and diatoms. Light captured by chlorophyll B and the carotenes is transferred to the chlorophyll A molecule for processing. Chlorophyll A is the "star" of photosynthesis.

Green Light

Green light has gotten a bad rap when it comes to photosynthesis. We've been told since we were children that plants look green to our eyes because they reflect green light. While partially true, plants don't reflect 100% of the green light they receive—some is absorbed and some is reflected. The reflected green light can be absorbed by another leaf; thus, green light scatters further into the garden's canopy than red and blue. Many plants absorb as much as 70% to 90% of the green light they are given.

Green light is absorbed deep within the leaf tissue by a group of compounds called carotenoids, among which lycopene and beta-carotene are most well-known. Carotenoids cause plant leaves to thicken, increasing their ability to capture more light. Also, should a plant begin to shut down chlorophyll absorption due to light overexposure, green light can continue to drive photosynthesis.

Another good reason for a bit of green in your LED grow light is to make using it easier on your eyes. Red, blue, and green are the primary colors of light; when they are mixed together in computer monitors and televisions, they can recreate every color including white. Including 5% to 10% green emitters in an LED grow light makes it easier for the gardener to see problems that might otherwise be masked by the light's purplish-pink color.

Infrared: Emerson Enhancement Effect

In 1957, Robert Emerson conducted experiments regarding what wavelengths most efficiently drive photosynthesis. He noticed that photosynthesis dramatically drops off at 680nm and above. This was considered strange since chlorophyll isolated in a beaker absorbs light well above this point. Photosynthesis reductions above 680nm became known as the "red drop effect."

This led Emerson to additional experiments showing that plants respond disproportionately to the combination of infrared light and red wavelengths. He observed a dramatic increase in photosynthesis rates when plants were exposed to red light and infrared light at the same time. This phenomenon became known as the "Emerson enhancement effect."

Why is this important? Emerson's experiments showed that using small amounts of infrared spectrum in combination with other reds can increase our yields. It's not often when one plus one equals an output greater than two! Be sure to look for an LED grow light that includes infrared spectra so you can benefit from this effect.

Far Red + Infrared = Bigger Harvests

Beyond Photosynthesis: Light Signaling

Understanding what wavelengths you need in an LED grow light can be a daunting task. Typical photosynthesis charts show the chlorophyll response curve at each wavelength within PAR spectrum, with some consideration given to what is absorbed by the different carotenoids. But there is more to the picture: other light spectra, commonly called signaling wavelengths, are also needed for healthy plant growth. Signaling wavelengths regulate plant growth as well as development processes such as controlling internodal stretching. While you can grow plants without them, plants grown without signaling spectra won't yield as heavily and may develop weak stalks and stems—not the best for the big, heavy harvests you desire.

Phytochrome

Phytochrome is an extremely important plant growth regulator that functions in the red end of the visible light spectrum. While it has no role in photosynthesis, phytochrome controls internodal elongation and flowering initiation (photoperiodism). The best understood of the plant-signaling compounds, phytochrome has two active states: phytochrome red (P_r) absorbs light around 650nm to 670nm, and phytochrome far red (P_{fr}) absorbs light at 705nm to 740nm. Note that the P_{fr} absorption is outside of the PAR spectrum range.

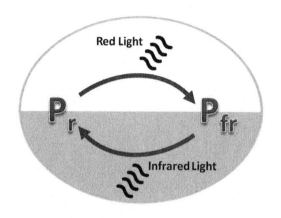

Phytochrome Red-Far Red Conversion

The ratio between P_r and P_{fr}, which convert back and forth depending on the light they receive, affects the plant's physical shape, including its height. Plants use phytochrome to sense infrared light hitting their stems, much of which passes straight through the leaves while the accompanying red light is absorbed by the leaves. To develop their normal shape, plants must receive specific ratios of red and infrared light on their stems; without enough infrared, the plants will sense that they are being blocked from the light and will stretch (increase internodal distance) to search for it.

Short-day plants, discussed in chapter 6, also rely on phytochrome to initiate flowering. Flowering begins when a sufficient quantity of P_{fr} converts back to the P_r form, a process that requires about 12 hours of uninterrupted darkness. That's why short-day plants grown outdoors begin to flower when day lengths shorten sometime after summer solstice, and it's why indoor growers switch to a 12-hours-on/12-hours-off light cycle for flowering short-day plants.

On the research front, growers have been experimenting with using phytochrome to extend "day" length during the flowering phase. Why lengthen the "day?" So that your plants have more time to turn light into sugars and so they can then use those sugars to grow stronger stems and bigger yields. Short-day plants generally require 12 hours to convert

P_{fr} to P_r. Growers have been able to increase yields by keeping the lights on for 13 or 14 hours then finishing the light cycle with infrared light only for periods ranging from a few seconds to a few minutes. This short period of infrared light jumpstarts the P_{fr}-to-P_r conversion process, allowing the plants to convert enough P_{fr} to P_r during a shortened night cycle to continue vigorous flowering. Some growers also report that this process allows them to grow the same-sized plants but harvest their crop a few days to weeks sooner than without the infrared exposure at lights out.

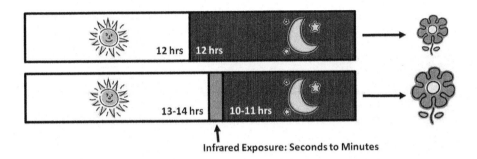

Day Length Extension Research

Cryptochrome

Cryptochrome is similar to phytochrome in that it's a photosensor, though it captures blue, violet and a small amount of UV-A light. While less understood than phytochrome, cryptochrome also assists in regulating the physical size and shape of plants, both alone and in combination with phytochrome. Cryptochrome affects the plant's "circadian clock," which is how the plant perceives night and day, as well as being responsible for phototropism—the process that causes plants to turn toward the light. Sunflowers provide an example of this effect: their flowers track the sun from the east in the morning to the west in the evening.

It's not necessary to search out an LED grow light with UV-A spectrum; in fact, it's safer for your eyes and skin if you don't. Most current LED grow lights have sufficient blue light to activate cryptochrome photosensors without added UV light.

UV Light

Ultraviolet light (UV) is often misunderstood. There are three bands of UV light: UV-A, UV-B, and UV-C. Each has different characteristics and therefore different applications. Much of the confusion about UV light stems from not understanding what UV light is and how it works. The following table helps to explain the differences.

	Wavelength	Applications	DNA effect	Other
UV-A	400–320nm "Long Wave"	Black light	Indirect DNA damage	Excites cryptochrome
UV-B	320–280nm "Medium Wave"	Reptile lamps, Phototherapy	Direct DNA damage	Causes sunburns
UV-C	200–280nm "Short Wave"	Germicidal	Direct DNA damage	Mostly filtered by the atmosphere, harmful

Table: UV Bands and Characteristics

If indoor gardeners supplement with UV light, it should to be UV-B. In some plants, UV-B is thought to increase flavonoids and terpenoids. Flavonoids are compounds that are responsible for many of the vibrant colors of the plant, which in nature help to attract beneficial insects that can aid in pollination. Flavonoids also inhibit certain plant pathogens. Terpenoids are responsible for aromatic plant smells. From eucalyptus trees to cinnamon, terpenoids are the compounds you smell.

When investigating LED grow lights that contain UV, find out from the manufacturer what wavelength of UV is used in the light. Some LED grow lights use inexpensive UV-A LEDs so they can say their products contain "UV light." Helpful UV-B LED emitters are still very expensive and so are less common in LED grow lights.

One way to add UV to your garden is to supplement your LED grow light with one or more UV tanning light(s). These generally emit a bit of UV-A along with UV-B and come in various sizes and output strengths, and they are generally a less-expensive solution than LED grow lights that include expensive UV-B emitters. Wear sunglasses when working under UV light to protect your eyes, and if you'll be working in the garden for a long time, consider applying sunscreen.

Too Much Light

As previously mentioned, we can exceed the light requirements of our plants with modern LED grow lights. When exposed to too much light intensity, plants shut down photosynthesis through a process called photoinhibition. Photoinhibition is a serious problem: not only are the plants not converting light into sugars so they can grow, they actually spend energy to defend themselves through a process called "feedback de-excitation" that disperses excess energy from over-stimulated chlorophyll molecules. Unfortunately, feedback de-excitation also releases dangerous free radicals inside the plant, which attack chlorophyll molecules and other structures within the plant.

Daily Light Integral

One way to understand what "too much light" means to plants is to learn about a total daily light limit called the "daily light integral" (DLI). The DLI is the total amount of light moles (1 million micromoles) received by a plant during a single light period. The maximum DLI that can be achieved outside in full sun is about 60 moles/day. This level should never be exceeded indoors.

Many commercially grown plants have published DLI limits. Take the time to look up the DLI for the plants you're growing indoors. Exceeding this limit can make the plants shut down and start spending energy to protect themselves instead of producing harvests. Over-lighting your garden is a waste—costly on the electric bills and harmful to your plants.

Use the equation below to calculate the DLI, measured in total micromoles per day, for your garden. The light used for this example provides 1000 micromoles of light intensity during a 12-hour photoperiod:

Micromoles per meter^2 per second $\mu mol/m^2/sec$	x 60 sec/min	x 60 min/hour	x photoperiod length hours/day	Micromoles per day $\mu mol/m^2/day$
1000	x 60	x 60	x 12	= 43,200,000

Divide by 1,000,000 to convert from micromoles to moles of light:

43,200,000 μmol/day ÷ 1,000,000 = 43.2 moles/day

5: Choosing an LED Grow Light

There's a lot to consider when buying an LED grow light: what type of garden you maintain, what you're growing, what type of light and spectrum that will work best for you, the type and quality of the emitters, where it's manufactured...sorting through these details can be daunting, even with everything you've learned so far. This chapter will help you cut through the clutter and make the best choice in LED grow lights for your garden and gardening style. There is a handy checklist at the end of the chapter to help you make this all-important garden purchase.

LED Grow Lights by Garden Type

The "right" or "best" LED grow light for your garden depends on your garden size and gardening goals. Consider these three types of gardens: hobbyist, small commercial, and large commercial.

	Hobbyist	Small Commercial	Large Commercial
Number of Lights	1–3	4–10	10+
LED Light Use	Primary	Supplemental	Photoperiod Extension
Space Used	Closet/Tent	Whole room(s)	Greenhouse(s)

Table: LED Grow Light Applications by Garden Type

Hobbyist

Hobbyists are small growers providing for their personal needs and/or those of their family members. They typically use one or two grow lights and have small gardens. LED grow lights are excellent as primary lighting for this application since they are so much easier to set up and use than HIDs. Not having to deal with excessive heat, ducting, and other heat-removing strategies makes LED grow lights perfect for small gardens. Anyone can grow their own with LED grow lights. If this is you, get over the initial cost and get growing with an LED grow light.

Small Commercial

The small commercial grower is typically growing as one of many suppliers to local markets or restaurants, or selling directly to consumers. They grow for personal need and sell the extra for profit. Small commercial growers use more lights and more grow space than the hobbyist and should consider LED grow lights for supplemental lighting. Used in addition to HIDs, LED grow lights can increase the quality of the plants and their harvest size. LEDs are also very useful for adding extra light in dark corners and at the side of the garden.

Commercial

Large-scale commercial growers that use grow lights typically garden in greenhouses and use 1000-watt HID grow lights to supplement natural daylight and extend day length. Commercial greenhouse operators need to conduct cost-benefit analyses comparing their electrical savings to the expenses of adding LED grow lights. Depending on electrical rates, LEDs can be a viable alternative for light supplementation in commercial greenhouses. A commercial grower considering LED grow lights should check with the manufacturer to be sure the light is designed for greenhouse use—a humid greenhouse environment could cause trouble for the wrong light.

Which Wavelengths?

The following table, which lists the light wavelengths most commonly absorbed by plants, is helpful when choosing a LED grow light. For each photo-reactive substance within a plant, the table lists the peak wavelength at which absorption is maximized, that compound's function within the plant, and the "color" of the light. This table can be useful when talking with LED grow light manufacturers about the light spectrum their lights provide.

	Peak Wavelength	Function	"Color"
Beta-Carotene	470nm	Signaling, Carbon Fixation	Blue
Chlorophyll A	465nm, 665nm	Carbon Fixation	Blue, Red "660"
Chlorophyll B	453nm, 642nm	Carbon Fixation	Blue, Red
Phycoeryththrin	495 and 545/566nm	Signaling	Aqua/Turquoise, Green
Phycocyanin	620nm	Signaling	Red
Cryptochrome	450nm, 370nm	Signaling, Light Quality	Dark Blue, UV
Phytochrome	P_r 660nm, P_{fr} 730nm	Signaling	Infrared, Red "660"

Table: Plant Photo-Active Substances and Spectra Absorbed

These photoactive compounds will absorb light not only at the listed peak wavelength, but also for some distance on either side of the peak and may also have secondary absorbance peaks. With that in mind, it's possible to find LED grow lights with emitters that stimulate most, if not all, of the known photoreceptors.

Before you buy an LED grow light, ask the manufacturer to provide you with the exact wavelengths in nanometers that their light produces. Don't accept answers such as "blue," "blue-green," "red," or "UV." Unfortunately, it's likely that you'll encounter LED grow light manufacturers who either don't know this information or are unwilling to disclose it. Should you run into one of them, run away.

Also ask the manufacturer for the number of and/or ratio between the various emitters included in a grow light. Look for lights that include as many spectra as possible out of the six wavelengths listed in the following table. The table on the next page shows an example of an LED emitter selection that works well for gardens with crops that demand high levels of light.

Wavelength	Color	Percent of LED Emitters (rounded up)
440–450nm	Dark Blue	10%
470nm	Blue	10%
525–540nm	Green	5%
620–640nm	Red	20%
660nm—*most important!*	Red 660	50%
725–740nm	Infrared	10%

Table: Example LED Emitter Selection for High-Light Crops

Another reason to learn the ratio of LED emitters included in a grow light you're considering is to verify that the manufacturer's claims about the light are represented in the light itself. For example, an LED grow light manufacturer can claim the light provides "660nm red light" if it includes only *one* 660nm emitter in the entire light. Unscrupulous manufacturers might try to skimp on this critical wavelength even though current research indicates that about half of the emitters in an LED grow light should be red 660s.

The perfect emitter wavelengths and ratio has not yet been perfected. The science behind photosynthesis is far from complete, and much of the information included in this book is newly discovered. It's quite possible that there are additional light-harvesting complexes in plants that are not known; we may need different wavelengths or ratios to excite them.

LED research is unlocking new mysteries all the time: there are always new theories, and manufacturers willing to build new lights based on them. Time will tell what works and what doesn't. You will need a light that strongly drives the carbon-fixing processes (blue, red, red 660) and contains some or all of the signaling wavelengths (dark blue, green, infrared). Considering the Emerson enhancement effect along with phytochrome's critical role in plant development, it would be wise to purchase a light that includes some infrared emitters.

White Light for You

The pinkish-purple hue of LED grow lights can hide many things you need to know about your plants, including nutrient deficiencies, bugs, and mildew. This is one problem LED gardeners have that HID gardeners don't. Some LED grow lights come with white emitters as part of their color blend. This might be enough for the task of examining your garden. If yours does not include white emitters, hang a small fluorescent light or two in the garden to help you see what you're missing. Don't get lazy and skip this part—this is experience talking.

Plug the fluorescent light(s) into a plug strip, extension cord, or socket that is controlled by your LED grow light timer and *not* directly into a wall socket, so it can't accidently be left on and interrupt the dark cycle. Anytime you suspect a problem, but not less than once a week, turn the LED grow light(s) off during the light cycle, and give your garden a careful inspection with just the white light on. Don't forget to turn the LED grow light back on after you're done.

Beam Angle

LED emitters all include an internal lens that controls the direction of the light that's emitted. These internal lenses are generally described by the angle of the light that streams out of the emitter, measured in degrees, known as the "beam angle." The smaller the beam angle, the more directly the light is focused downward. So-called "narrow" beam angles are typically less than 60 degrees. A narrow beam angle causes the area directly beneath the LED grow light to be strongly illuminated, but the light will not spread outside of the grow light's actual physical size. Larger beam angles spread the light out more, providing less intense light directly beneath the LED grow light but with a spread that exceeds the emitter's size. Typically these lens angles are 60 to 120 degrees.

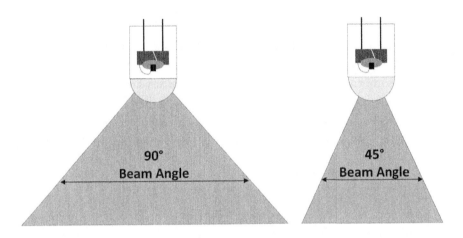

LED Beam Angle

Your garden goals will dictate what the best beam angle is for you. If growing tall plants, look for narrow beam angles. If you're growing shorter or wider plants, consider wider beam angles.

Secondary Optics

We've already discussed how secondary optics take the light generated from an emitter and its internal lens to the next level by focusing and intensifying the light. It's truly amazing how much the light from an LED grow light can be intensified when the correct LED is paired up to the correct secondary optical lens. Gone are the days when LED grow lights only illuminated the space below them with mediocre-quality light. Secondary optics are one of the developments that have really put LED grow lights into the fast lane.

The real-world drive behind developing secondary optics for LEDs is to develop lights that are bright enough and cover large enough areas to replace incandescent lamps in our homes, offices, and public spaces. They also help to change the look of LED lights from ugly-looking "dots of light" into more traditional-looking fixtures, including direct replacements for certain types of incandescent bulbs. We growers benefit from this research.

You can recognize LED grow lights with secondary optics because their light panel doesn't look like a whole bunch of emitters stuck into a sheet of metal, sometimes under glass. Secondary lenses are made from optical plastic and come in many shapes and sizes, but generally you can't see the LEDs themselves—just a clear, curved, or faceted plastic cover. Purchasing a LED grow light with secondary optics is recommended.

Heat Sinks

Except for chemical light sources such as glow sticks and red tides, creating light also creates heat. And so, like all electrically driven light sources, high-powered LEDs used in grow lights require cooling. High operating temperatures cause LED lights to emit fewer photons and can dramatically reduce the lifespan of the lights. Overheated LEDs can also shift their output wavelength so that the light no longer delivers the advertised spectrum. Since we specifically chose the wavelengths we wanted our plants to receive when we bought our LED grow lights, it would be silly to screw it all up by not removing the light's heat properly.

The best way to cool LED grow lights is with a heat sink: a metal block inside the grow light that absorbs then radiates the light's heat into the surrounding air. Generally, you need about 10 square inches of heat sink surface area, open to free air, per LED watt. For example, to properly cool a 300-watt LED grow light, the heat sink should provide 3,000 square inches of surface area—a huge area if it were flat, which is why heat sinks have fan-like shapes that provide a lot of surface area in a small package.

To save costs, some LED grow lights feature undersized heat sinks—somewhere between three and six inches per watt. Then air is blown across the heat sink by a fan to dissipate the excess heat. This design can produce "false savings": not only is the heat sink inadequately sized to remove enough heat, it also introduces an unnecessary failure point with the fan. A failed fan on a light with an inadequate heat sink will cause the light to overheat and could damage the light. Don't be fooled—select a light with a big enough heat sink.

Drivers

LED grow lights don't have ballasts like HID lights. Instead, they use "drivers" to supply the correct voltage and current (amperage) to the LEDs. Physically, a driver can be a simple resistor or a complicated, constant current driver made up of numerous electronic components. LED grow lights may have multiple drivers to separately control various colors or banks of emitters within the light.

Resistor-based drivers are inexpensive components that produce a fixed voltage and current. These components are sensitive to temperature change, so with a resistor-based driver, as the internal temperature of the grow light increases, the light output will decrease. These drivers may have been fine before high-powered LED emitters hit the market, but with today's LED grow lights, resistor-based drivers are inadequate.

Constant current drivers are more costly but superior. These drivers produce a constant voltage and current regardless of the surrounding temperature, due to sensing circuits that allow the driver to accommodate the effect of temperature changes. LEDs driven by constant current drivers produce consistent brightness levels regardless of temperature fluctuations.

LED Emitters

LED "BIN" Codes

When it comes to LEDs, the term BIN is an acronym for Brightness Index Number. It's a multi-digit number that indicates the LED's brightness and color rating. Many people are confused about this term, thinking that BIN means a physical sorting bin instead of an abbreviation. They may believe that a "higher BIN" is physically above a "lower BIN" on a shelf or rack.

Unfortunately, not all LEDs emitters are created equal. Wide quality variances arise during the LED manufacturing process, partly because of raw material quality differences. The LED manufacturing process ends with testing the output of each batch, measured as BIN. This testing requirement is one of the scale problems facing LED manufacturers: it's expensive and time consuming to test each batch, but current manufacturing processes and raw material quality don't leave them any choice. The testing process results in emitters being separated into different quality classes and assigned BIN codes that describe varying quality levels of the "same" emitter. The actual codes change from manufacturer to manufacturer.

What this really means is that the same "1-watt red LED emitter" from Manufacturer X can have significantly different outputs, in both color and brightness. Unscrupulous LED light manufacturers have been known to produce demonstration units with high-quality emitters and then switch to cheaper emitters for their production products. While there's really no way to know without expensive test equipment whether the grow light you're buying was made with high- or low-quality emitters, you can protect yourself by buying only from reputable LED grow light manufacturers and suppliers.

3watt/3 Explained

In LED grow lights, there's a trade-off between electrical efficiency and the ability of the emitted light to penetrate into the garden canopy. For example, let's compare 1-watt versus 3-watt emitters. One-watt LEDs are efficient in terms of photons per watt, but they lack the punch to penetrate light into the canopy of larger plants. Three-watt LEDs offer better penetration but emit less photons per watt consumed.

When considering LED grow lights that claim to include 2- or 3-watt LEDs, make sure you understand what you're actually getting. If the LED emitters in the light are labeled "2watt/2" or "3watt/3," this means that two or three 1-watt emitters have been placed under a single lens and are being *called* higher wattage emitters. This is misleading to the uninformed. Three emitters under a single lens generate more heat than a true 3-watt emitter, limiting the electrical wattage the combined emitter can handle, which in turn lowers the amount of light the "3watt/3" LED can produce.

For example, true 3-watt LED emitters typically consume 700 milliamps (mA) of power, but a 3watt/3 emitter is limited to 550mA—a reduction of over 20%. Compound emitters made up of multiple 1-watt emitters won't ever produce as much light as the true 2- or 3-watt emitters they are trying to mimic. Compound emitters have their place in LED grow lights: they're cheaper and can be just fine for small gardens. Just be aware and wary about what you're buying.

When 200 Watts Is 300 Watts

As if it was not complicated enough to choose an LED grow light, LED manufacturers use different specifications to describe their lights. The power level of LED grow lights is often advertised as either the amount of "wall watts" consumed (energy drawn from an electrical outlet), the number of LEDs in the light multiplied by their maximum allowable power, or some other totally made up number. For example, an LED grow light with 100 3-watt emitters that uses 200 wall watts could be advertised as either a 200- or 300-watt LED grow light. Wall watts are the most reliable measure of LED grow light power levels—or at least the most important when it comes to not overloading an electric circuit.

Why does this matter? Most of the time, it doesn't—your garden doesn't care what yardstick the manufacturer uses in a marketing pitch. Be sure to ask the manufacturer what method is use to describe the power level of a specific light so you can plan accordingly.

LED Grow Light Designs

LED grow lights come in four basic designs: a single surface covered with emitters, light heads with multiple emitters under the same lens, lights with clusters or "rosettes" of emitters, and tube lights that resemble fluorescent lamps, some of which can be used in regular fluorescent light fixtures.

Single-Surface LED Grow Lights

Single-surface LED grow lights look like someone loaded up a shotgun and blasted LED emitters across a flat metal sheet. Some LED grow lights feature densely emitters packed across the entire downward surface of the grow light while others space them out. These lights may or may not include secondary optics in the design.

- Advantages: These square- or rectangular-shaped grow lights provide even illumination that conforms to the shape of many indoor gardens.
- Disadvantages: If one driver or bank of LEDs fails, the entire light potentially becomes useless. No ability for the end user to customize or upgrade the wavelengths—you're stuck with what's in the light at the time of manufacture. The units must be sent in for repair.
- What to look for: Large heat sink backed up with fans to dissipate the heat concentrated by so many closely mounted LEDs.

LED Light Heads

In sharp contrast to flat-surface grow lights are LED grow lights shaped as individual light heads that pack multiple emitters under a single lens. LED light heads can be used individually or mounted on a fixed or spinning chassis. Many of these lights offer targeted wavelengths for specific growth purposes such as vegetative, bloom booster, and daylight. Heat sinks are also a critical feature of these lights. Typically the body of the light extends the size of the heat sink, so additional cooling fans are not required.

- Advantages: Easily customize shape, light volume, and wavelengths by purchasing separate light heads. If one head fails, the other heads are not affected, and only the nonworking head needs to be replaced.
- Disadvantages: Multiple, separate heads can create complex lighting setups in large gardens. Bulky mounting hardware may be required, potentially increasing the vertical height of the garden. Spinning mounts to "mix" the light colors can be complex to hang, can consume additional wattage, and can create a new potential failure point in the garden as well as add additional costs.
- What to look for: Light heads with advertised light output in both wavelength and micromoles, so you can purchase the correct number of light heads to meet your garden's daily light integral and spectral needs. Easy mounting setup.

Clusters/Rosettes

Arranging the LEDs into clusters is another option in reflector design and was among the first LED grow light designs to hit the market. In these lights, lots of LEDs are closely packed together, with spaces between the clusters. Think of them as portholes on a ship, where the emitter groups are the holes and they are evenly spaced apart down the length of the ship. Some manufacturers mount their clusters inside a metal box while others mount them on bars, with multiple bars typically used to customize light coverage for the garden.

- Advantages: On some units, if one cluster fails it can be removed and replaced by the end user. Clusters can be upgraded if the manufacturer introduces improved spectra or higher light output.
- Disadvantages: Not all lights that employ clusters are end-user replaceable/upgradeable.
- What to look for: End-user replaceable clusters. Even cluster spacing for optimum coverage. Correct beam angles to match garden shape.

Tube-Style LED Bars

Tube style LED lights are long tubes similar to a fluorescent lamp but filled with LEDs. Most are approximately the size of a T8 fluorescent lamp. They come equipped with internal voltage regulation, so there is no need for an external ballast. Be sure to use ONLY the fluorescent lighting fixtures recommended by the manufacturer—standard fluorescent fixtures with their own ballast can destroy the LED tube. If the LED tube manufacturer doesn't specify a particular lighting fixture, then use fixtures that are directly wired, with the ballast removed. If you are unfamiliar with this type of work, consult an electrician.

- Advantages: Square or rectangular shape of tube-style grow light fixtures mimics the size and shape of many indoor gardens. If one tube fails, the others are unaffected. Some light fixtures on the market combine LED and fluorescent grow light tubes, which can enhance performance over fluorescent grow lights used alone. They are perfect for supplemental lighting.
- Disadvantages: Currently LED grow light tubes are typically red only or blue only and do not include many of the wavelengths plants need, particularly signaling spectra and infrared.
- What to look for: Tubes that provide all of the wavelengths needed to produce healthy plants, including 440–460nm (dark blue), 470nm (blue), 525–540nm (green), 620–640nm (red), 660nm (red 660) and 725–740nm (infrared).

"Chainable" Lights

Most of the newer LED grow lights can be chained together, which means that several lights can be connected together to use one electrical wall outlet. If an LED grow light is chainable, the manufacturer will specify how many can be chained together. NEVER exceed the recommended number of chained lights, or you risk overloading the circuitry. When chaining grow lights together, use zip ties or Velcro straps to keep the cords between lights out of the way.

- Advantages: Simplifies grow room setup and allows you to use one timer to turn all the lights on or off at the same time.
- Disadvantages: If one light fails, it might bring the whole chain down with it. This varies between lights, depending on how they are wired. For this reason, some growers prefer to plug multiple lights into a plug strip then plug the strip into a single timer.
- What to look for: Chainable lights with UL or EC certification, to ensure they can handle the extra electrical load. Lights with secure cord connectors that will not dislodge easily.

How Many LED Grow Lights Does My Garden Need?

How many lights to use is one of the million-dollar questions. If you're converting from HID lighting, start with one or more LED grow lights that consume somewhere near 50% to 60% of HID watts currently being used. For example, if you're currently gardening with a 600-watt HID light, you should look at LED grow lights that draw at least 300 to 350 watts of electricity. This ratio will change as better, more efficient LEDs and optics are developed. Contact the manufacturer to verify that this assumption holds valid for your gardening needs.

If you're not currently gardening with an HID light, then start by consulting with the LED manufacturer or the owners' manual for the light you're considering. All LED grow lights are different: wattage, emitters, and lens configuration all affect the light's coverage area.

The size and shape of your grow space will also affect the size and number of LED grow lights you need. If you're gardening in a closet that's 2.5 by 5 feet, you may find that two 200-watt LED grow lights hung in a line will cover your canopy better than one 400-watt grow light hung in the center. This is part of the fun of LED gardening—learning about and thinking through all of the options available to make the best choice for your garden.

Types of LED Grow Light Suppliers

LED grow lights are a sizeable investment so do your homework. Try to learn as much about the manufacturer as you can when making this investment. Take the time to email simple questions and see how complete of an answer you get as well as how long it takes for the response. Alternatively give them a call and discuss the light you're considering. The better manufacturers will have a customer support line. LED grow light manufacturers fall into four basic types:

Large, Well-Funded Company

Well-funded companies that produce or distribute LED grow lights on a large scale are the preferred type of LED grow light supplier. They usually have strong relationships with their vendors and so have access to get top-quality components. These grow light suppliers can quickly send out a replacement or loaner light if there's a problem. They are likely to have support staff available to take phone calls, and they can ship in a timely manner. On the other hand, well-established LED grow light suppliers may not be able to adapt to change as fast as smaller companies. They may need to burn through existing stock before making changes to their lights.

Small Importer or Manufacturer

When this book was written, most LED grow light suppliers were small, often underfunded companies. These early-stage companies build or import small lots of grow lights without much in the way of inventory reserves or spares. They tend to deliver slowly—you may end up waiting for them to receive critical components before they can build your light. Some of these manufacturers produce top-quality lights and have the support to back them up, but some don't. Use your gut when considering one of their lights. Will they be in business long enough to support their warranty? Can they deliver to your expectations? If you can live with some uncertainty but feel good about them, go for it. You may discover a great light at a great price.

Drop Ship Direct

Companies that drop ship direct from overseas LED grow light manufacturers, instead of maintaining their own inventory, are generally "me too" players trying to ride the LED wave and make a fast buck without putting a significant amount of their own capital at risk. These suppliers generally have limited technical expertise and may not be able to answer basic questions about indoor gardening or the lights they distribute. The two concerns in dealing with these companies are the quality of their products, particularly the emitters, and shipping timeliness. They also have limited customer service abilities—if your light breaks, you generally have to ship it back to where it was made (likely overseas, which is potentially expensive and slow), wait for a repair, and then wait again for the grow light to be shipped back. This can take several weeks—can your garden survive that long without light? Probably not. Unfortunately this type of supplier is becoming more common. If you can identify one, run away. Remember, there are a lot of very clever Internet sites that look great but are not the real deal.

You the Reader (Homebuilt)

Then there's the classic "DIY" homebuilt LED grow light. Someone put lots of life energy into producing what they considered to be the perfect light. How good are these lights? That all depends on how they were built and with what components. You should meticulously go through the "Selecting an LED Grow Light Checklist" at the end of this before building an LED grow light or buying a home built one. One of the best things about DIY grow lights is that they can often be changed as technology evolves—since you built it or know who did, you're in a great position to resolve issues and upgrade your light. If you're handy with a soldering iron, go for it—your LED grow light might be a game changer.

My Light Failed—Now What?

Any type of grow light can fail; what happens should your grow light fail is one of the most of the overlooked buying criteria. Overcoming a failed grow light is more difficult in LED-based gardens than HID gardens since it's cost prohibitive to keep a spare LED light sitting around "just in case." Switching back to an HID light mid-grow presents all sorts of problems, since you use different gardening techniques with LED grow lights.

For any grow light you're considering, ask the manufacturer to answer the questions listed below in order to "vet" their ability to help you should the light fail. Make sure you're talking to the actual manufacturer instead of a distributor such as a retail or online hydroponic equipment shop. While these distributors may be the only places where you can buy an LED grow light, they can only convey the information provided to them by the light's manufacturer—which may not include the answers you need. When you're getting serious about buying an LED grow light, make sure you get straight and believable answers to these questions:

- Where was the light made? Where is it repaired?
- Will the manufacturer send a loaner? Does the manufacturer require a deposit? How and when is the deposit refunded?
- Who pays for shipping, both to the repair facility and then back to you?
- Who owns manufacturing responsibilities, quality control, and customer support?
- Why do you think you will be in business in one, two, or three years in order to make good on your warranty?

Checklist: Selecting an LED Grow Light

Garden Type
- ❏ Hobbyist: LED grow lights as primary
- ❏ Small Commercial: HID primary, LEDs supplemental
- ❏ Commercial: LEDs as supplemental light in greenhouse

Wavelengths, in nm
- ❏ 440–460 Dark Blue
- ❏ 470 Blue
- ❏ 525–540 Green
- ❏ 620–640 Red
- ❏ 660 "Red 660"
- ❏ 725–740 Infrared

Lens Options
- ❏ Beam Angle: Narrow or Wide
- ❏ Secondary Optics?

Heat Sink
- ❏ Surface area size in square inches
- ❏ Exposed to the air?
- ❏ Backup fan?

Drivers
- ❏ Type: Constant Current or Resistor
- ❏ How many?
- ❏ What do they control?

Emitters
- ❏ Emitter wattage
- ❏ Emitter type: Single or Multiple emitters/ single lens
- ❏ If multiple, wattage & how many?

Grow Light Wattage	❑ How are grow light watts computed? Wall watts or total of emitters?
Light Design	❑ Single-surface ❑ Individual light heads with multiple emitters ❑ Clusters or "rosettes" of emitters ❑ LED tube
Chainable	❑ Yes or No
How Many?	_____ Square footage of garden space being illuminated _____ Micromoles of light your garden needs (daily light integral) _____ Micromoles of light produced at recommended hanging height _____ Manufacturer recommended coverage area
Supplier Type	❑ Large company, large-scale importer or manufacturer ❑ Small company, small-scale importer or manufacturer ❑ Direct drop ship from foreign suppliers ❑ Homebuilt, hobby, or DIY

6. Growing with LEDs

It takes a bit of practice to grow effectively with LED garden lights—just like it does when using any garden light. Why shouldn't it? If you're learning to garden indoors for the first time using LED grow lights, the advice in this book should be very helpful to get started, and with a little experience you should be off and running. If you're converting from HIDs, you'll need to make many changes to your gardening technique—most small but significant—to achieve the best yields possible.

Plant Types

Short-Day versus Day-Neutral versus Long-Day Plants

The most important decision to make about using your LED grow light is how long to keep the lights on. This choice depends on what you're growing. The best photoperiod, or length of time the lights are on, is different for different types of plants—and for different stages in a plant's life cycle. Biologists have come up with a classification system based on plant photoperiod requirements: short-day, day-neutral, and long-day plants.

	Short-Day	Day-Neutral	Long-Day
When plant flowers or fruits	When nights get longer (fall)	Independent of photoperiod	When nights get shorter (spring)
Example	Cotton, Rice, Hemp	Roses, Tomatoes, Cucumbers	Spinach, Lettuce, Grasses
Photoperiod	12 hours or less	Independent	14–18 hours

Table: Short-Day, Day-Neutral and Long-Day Plants

Don't let the names confuse you. Even though these categories are defined by how long the "day" is, it's really all about the dark. Scientists originally thought that day length was what triggered plants to fruit or flower, but further research has taught us that it's the length of the night or dark cycle that stimulates hormonal responses within plants that initiate flowering.

Short-day/long-night plants begin to form fruits or flowers as day length shortens and night length increases—sometime after summer solstice. These plants include fall-blooming flowers and fall-producing crops such as poinsettia, chrysanthemum, cotton, rice, and hemp.

Many plants don't care about day length and are therefore called "day neutral." These plants automatically fruit or flower when they get to a certain size or age, or when temperatures or humidity reach a certain range. Tulips, tomatoes, and many trees are day neutral.

Long-day/short-night plants initiate flowering when the nights begin to shorten—10 to 12 hours of darkness with longer days. Many common vegetables and flowers are long-day plants such as lettuce, radish, spinach, potatoes, sunflowers, and daisies.

So what does this mean to you? For short-day plants, grow them up from seeds or cuttings with the lights on 18–20 hours a day, then change to a 12-hour-a-day light period to initiate flowering. For day-neutral plants, set the lights to run for 18 hours a day and forget them. For long-day plants, grow them up with 12 hours of light then change to 18–20 hours of light to flower. Give all plants uninterrupted darkness when the lights are off.

To be clear: uninterrupted darkness means NO LIGHT at all. Small pin-hole light leaks, light entering through the seam of a grow tent, or light admitted when "I just want to poke my head in for a second and check on something" is NOT the same as uninterrupted darkness. Breaking the dark cycle can stall flowering and may cause the plants to revert to vegetative growth. Don't do it.

C3, C4, and CAM Plant Types

Plants are also classified by their method of acquiring CO_2 and the type of sugars they create during photosynthesis. These groupings are called C3, C4, and CAM.

C3

Ninety-five percent of all plants on the planet, including most plants grown in indoor gardens, are "C3" plants. In addition to having woody stems and rounded leaves, these plants produce a compound that includes three carbon atoms as the product of photosynthesis—hence the name C3. C3 plants eat up supplemental CO_2 like candy, speeding up their photosynthetic process, which makes more sugars available for growth. C3 plants open their stomata, small pores on the underside of their leaves, during the day to take CO_2 directly from the air.

What happens if the level of CO_2 in the air drops too low? C3 plants begin "binding" oxygen (O_2) instead of CO_2, a process known as "photorespiration." Photorespiration is a wasteful process that burns up the plant's energy without producing usable sugars and creates ammonia in the plant's cells as a byproduct.

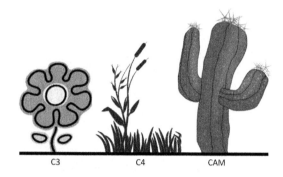

C3, C4 and CAM Plants

Then the plant has to waste even more energy to remove the excess ammonia: a distraction from what they should be doing—converting carbon and light into sugars in order to grow big harvests.

C4

"C4" plants produce a post-photosynthesis molecule that contains four carbon atoms, and they are mostly grasses, including corn and other cereal grains. C4 plants store the extra carbon atom in an intermediate internal holding site, so they don't take all of their carbon as CO_2 from the air. Because of this, the C4 photosynthetic process is a lot more efficient than the C3 process—by up to six times. C4 plants keep their stomata closed and only open them when they need to refill their carbon stores. Thus, C4 plants don't benefit very much from CO_2 supplementation as they have a built-in method to supplement carbon themselves.

CAM

Plants that fall into the crassulacean acid metabolism (CAM) grouping are typically desert plants such as cacti and succulents. They open their stomata at night to collect CO_2 instead of during the day. Similar to C4 plants, CAM plants make a four-carbon sugar as their photosynthesis output. These plants are not typically grown indoors under artificial lighting.

Maintaining the Environment

Maintaining a healthy indoor environment is critical to garden success. You can have the best plant genetics, space-age plant nutrition, and the greatest LED grow light ever, but if your environment is off, it will cost you in terms of quantity and quality. Heat-stressed, CO_2-deficient gardens just don't perform well.

For each stage of a plant's life cycle, there are suggested optimum environmental conditions. Don't worry if you can't get to these exact figures—they are recommendations, not requirements. We all have to deal with the real environment in our grow spaces and may not be able to pay for all the equipment needed to overcome its challenges. Do the best you can, and don't stress too much about being a few points off here and there.

The three basic environmental factors for any garden—indoors or out—are temperature, humidity, and CO_2 level. All three of these variables need to be at their optimum level for a garden to perform its best. Here's a quick rundown on how to create optimal conditions in your garden and how to make corrections if these factors are out of spec.

 Sloper Says

Don't spend too much time trying to "chase the number" on your thermometer/hygrometer. Instead, use the thermometer/hygrometer as a reference, watch your plants, and only intervene when there are problems.

Too Hot

Just like humans, plants suffer if the garden is too hot. Plants have evolved mechanisms to help them with too hot conditions: in the presence of sufficient water, plants cool themselves by opening their stomata and re-leasing water molecules that cool the plant as they evaporate. Plants can also reorientate the angle of their leaves limiting their exposure to the light. Both of these solutions require the plant to spend its energy defending itself instead of producing fruits and flowers. Additionally, chemical reactions inside a plant, including photosynthesis, depend on enzymes that operate best at particular temperatures and might stop working altogether outside of their target range.

What's too hot? In general, gardens thrive in the same conditions people do. "Daytime" or light-cycle temps should be in the mid-70s to mid-80s degrees Fahrenheit, though LED gardens can actually thrive into the lower 90s.

To cool down your grow space, consider these options:

- Fans are the most cost-effective heat-removing tool for an indoor garden. If the exhaust fan does not provide adequate cooling, consider adding an intake fan. Actively bringing air into the garden reduces back pressure on the exhaust fan and allows more air to flow out. If that doesn't reduce temperatures enough, consider buying a bigger exhaust fan. Both of these techniques assume that the outside air is cooler than the desired garden temperature.
- If fans are not enough, use an air conditioner. Since air conditioners are expensive to operate, look for ones with SEER (Seasonal Energy Efficiency Ratio) ratings of 13 or greater. If you're supplementing with CO_2, be sure to use an A/C that separates the room air from the exhaust air—such as a "dual hose" unit or a "mini-split."

Too Cold

Too cold is one problem HID gardeners rarely encounter. While excess heat is a perpetual threat to the HID garden, LED gardens can get too cold, even during the light cycle. Extended periods of daytime temperatures below 65°F can stunt growth and shrink harvests. Too cold isn't generally much of a problem during the summer, but it can be a serious challenge in winter, depending on where you live.

To warm up your grow space, consider these options:

- Heaters are useful, though they draw a significant amount of electricity. When using a heater with a fan, be careful to not blow hot air directly onto the plants or you can burn them or dry them out. Oil-filled radiator-style heaters are better, as they radiate heat into the room without blowing it around.
- Use a fan speed controller to automatically speed up or slow down the exhaust fan based on room temperature. Fan speed controllers are a cost-effective alternative to expensive environmental controllers. Choose a controller that changes the fan's rotation based on temperature: lower temp = slower fan speed. This helps retain existing heat in the grow space.
- If the area immediately outside of the grow space is warmer, crack the door open during the light cycle to let some of the warm outside air mix in with the cooler air in the garden.
- Consider using a backdraft dampener to prevent any unwanted airflow into the garden through stopped intake or exhaust fans.

Too Humid

Proper humidity is just as important to successful gardening as proper temps. When your garden is too humid, it is at risk of attack by fungus and mold that can ruin your whole garden and contaminate your harvest. Fungus is very hard to kill and multiplies exponentially, so every hour matters. In addition, when it's overly humid, the plants have difficulty transpiring.

Transpiration is the name for the process by which moisture is moved from the roots to the leaves then released into the atmosphere. It occurs when a plant opens its stomata and release water molecules. In addition to cooling the plant, transpiration enables the movement of water through capillary action. When it's humid, transpiration efficiency is significantly decreased.

"Too humid" varies from garden to garden. In general, ideal garden humidity is 50% plus or minus 10%, with "high humidity" beginning somewhere above 60%. What's ideal for your garden depends on many factors, including plant size, volume of airflow, average temperatures, and the type of growing system you use. Pay attention and don't let garden humidity get out of control.

To reduce humidity, try one of these tactics:

- If you can, raise garden temperature by a few degrees. Warmer air retains more water vapor, so as long as you have not introduced more water vapor into the grow space, relative humidity will drop as temps rise.
- If the air outside of the garden is dryer than the garden air, increase the number of air exchanges in your grow space by beefing up your ventilation system. This works best when outside air is about the same temperature as the air in your grow space—if not, you may need to find ways to correct garden temperature after bringing in more outside air.
- Dehumidifiers physically remove unwanted humidity from the air by blowing air across chilled plates or coils that condense water vapor in the air into water, which is collected in a vessel. The units turn on when humidity in the room exceeds a set point programmed by the gardener. If you're battling high temps, use a water-cooled dehumidifier instead of a "heat pump" model. Water-cooled units blow room-temperature air across a coil that's chilled by pumping cold water though it.
- Air conditioners dry out the air as a by-product of cooling it, solving two problems if your garden is also too hot. Just make sure you have a plan to remove and dispose of the water that condenses out of the air conditioner, as it can be fairly acidic. Don't use it to water living plants—it belongs down the drain.

Too Dry

Too dry can be just as devastating as too humid for some plants. Too dry is a lot like too hot: the plants close their stomata to protect themselves, shutting themselves down and slowing growth. Generally, this is more of a problem under HID lights than LEDs because of the excess heat produced by HIDs.

While more research on the topic is required, LED-grown plants seem to have a wider humidity tolerance than plants grown under other lights. At the top end, peak humidity is the same for all indoor gardens—not more than 60% to avoid growing fungus and mold. But at the low end of the scale, LED gardens are more tolerant, thriving with daytime humidity lows of 25–30%. A humidifier may no longer be required if you live in a dry climate—experiment and see.

To raise humidity, consider these techniques:

- Humidifiers spray fine water droplets into the air. The more expensive ultrasonic models spray a cool, fine mist in contrast to the large water droplets that impeller-style units spray out. With humidifiers, you get what you pay for: ultrasonic units are more expensive but raise the room's humidity more effectively than impeller units, without leaving water puddles wherever they stand.
- Small gardeners may be able to use the steam from a nearby shower for short-term humidification. This only works if the air supply to the garden is close to the bathroom.
- One or more wet towels hung in a small grow room can provide instant relief for a dry spell. This is a short-term solution—the towels must always be damp and so must be checked or changed several times a day. To prevent humidity buildup when the light is off, either let the towels dry out late in the day or remove them before the lights go out.

Low CO_2

These are several ways to increase the amount of CO_2 in your garden: intake/exhaust fans, CO_2 supplementation using tanks or CO_2 generators, and organic/chemical CO_2 emitters. Regardless of the method you choose, be sure to dispense the gas as high in the room as possible. CO_2 is denser than air so it will fall down on the plants. Releasing CO_2 at the same level as the plants may cause it to be wasted when it falls to the floor and stays there instead of contacting the plants' leaves where the photosynthetic magic happens.

Here are a few points to consider when it comes to maintaining or increasing CO_2 in your garden:

- Exhaust fans not only remove heat, they also replenish CO2 by bringing fresh outside air into the garden. This should ensure an adequate supply of fresh CO2 and is the best option for small gardeners who don't want to fuss with CO2 tanks or generators.
- The most common way to add CO_2 to your garden environment is to inject it from a pressurized tank. CO_2 tanks can be purchased at retail hydroponic shops and either exchanged at the shop when they are empty or refilled at a commercial gas distributor. CO_2 tanks need to be pressure checked every five years by law; check the inspection date stamped into the shoulder of the tank to be sure that it's "in-date." You'll also need a regulator for the tank, a timer or an electronic CO_2 controller to control the CO_2 release and maintain an appropriate CO_2 concentration, and a distribution system to scatter the CO_2 across the garden.
- CO_2 generators release CO_2 into the garden as a by-product of burning propane or natural gas. These units contain gas burner jets inside an insulated housing and when properly used present very little fire hazard. The gas burners are tuned to produce CO_2—safe carbon dioxide—rather than CO—dangerous carbon monoxide, which is a normal by-product of burning fossil fuels. While there is a risk that these units will produce a least a little CO, a dangerous accumulation in the garden is unlikely as long as the garden's ventilation system functions properly and the generator is in good working order. Be sure to put a CO alarm in your garden so you can identify CO buildup and take corrective action before the problem becomes dangerous to you and your plants. While you're at it, put

up a smoke alarm or combination smoke/CO alarm, and put a fire extinguisher in or near the garden.

- Compost and chemical bags are small buckets of mushroom compost or bags of chemicals that slowly release CO_2. Again position the outlet for these products as high in the garden as possible. Compost and chemical CO_2 generators are gaining in popularity for small gardens that don't have space for additional equipment, though the low CO_2 production of some of them makes one wonder "Why bother?" Try these buckets/bags if you're ready to experiment with CO_2 in a small garden, and see whether they help. It's likely that you'll need a CO_2 tank or burner along with a quality CO_2 environmental controller if you want to take the best advantage of supplemental CO_2 in your garden.

	Tank	Generator	Compost/Chemical
CO_2 Source	Cylindrical storage tank	Gas burners release CO_2 by burning propane or natural gas inside an insulated housing.	Decomposition
Gas Delivery Temperature	Cold Potential freeze hazard if the CO_2 regulator runs too long. If so, consider a CO_2 heater.	Hot Heat and water vapor released as by-products. Consider a water-cooled CO_2 generator if too hot or humid.	Room temperature
Need to Refill	Yes More than once a week in a large or unsealed room	Yes When using bottled propane	Refill or replace when exhausted.
Fire Hazard	No CO_2 is used in fire extinguishers.	Potential fire hazard	No
Grow Room Size	Small to medium	Medium to large	Small to very small

Table: Supplemental CO_2 Sources

Leaf Temp versus Wall Temp

Measuring garden temperatures accurately is not as easy as it seems. Be suspicious when someone brags that his or her garden stays a perfect 75°F all the time—how do they know? Most gardeners depend on a combination thermometer/hygrometer placed somewhere in the garden, which measures both temperature and relative humidity. Many also record high and low values. Elite gardeners use devices that provide a 24-hour recording of temps and humidity. All of these gardeners believe that their recording sensors tell them exactly what's happening in their gardens—but do they?

In a word, *no*. Most garden temperature devices are hung on the wall or receive input from a long-wired sensor that's suspended over the garden in a single spot. Moving that sensor up and down a few inches to a foot will change the measurement, possibly by quite a bit. If you're using one of these sensors, try moving it six inches in any direction—the results may surprise you. It's almost as though you should ask yourself: what temp do you want it to read?

While a temperature/humidity monitor can provide a good *indication* of what's happening in the garden, there's a lot more to the story. The temperature at the wall can vary significantly from the temperature of the plants' leaves. Leaf temp is what really matters.

The best way to understand leaf temperatures, aka "what the plants are feeling", is to use an infrared temp gun to take multiple measurements in different parts of the grow room and different parts of the plants. Observe temperatures throughout your grow space, and pay attention to variations between readings. Temps will naturally be higher near the top of the garden and lower near the bottom, since heat rises. If you discover hot or cold spots at the same "altitude", such as between plants that stand right next to each other, you may have discovered areas that are not getting sufficient air movement. Try moving the plants around or changing fan locations to even out the temps.

A high-tech tool for managing garden temperatures is a wireless sensor system. These systems can help you understand temperatures throughout your garden by collecting readings from several remote sensors that can be positioned anywhere in the garden. Once you've gained a comprehensive understanding of the temperatures in your garden and have equalized temperatures as well as you can, then a standard, wall-mounted temperature sensor is useful to advise you of macro changes that may signal an emerging problem.

Stages of Plant Growth

There are three basic stages of a plant's life: a seedling or clone, vegetative growth, and the fruiting/flowering stage. As summarized in the table at the end of the chapter, during each stage of their life, plants need different environmental conditions. This book assumes that you're growing C3 short-day plants, since these are the plants most commonly grown indoors.

Cloning/Seed Starting with LEDs

Clones and seedlings have very similar environmental needs. Growing from seed is just like it sounds—put a seed into a grow media of choice and feed/water it as necessary. Cloning is the process of taking a shoot from a donor plant and rooting it. Cloning allows for exact copies of the donor plant to be grown, so start with the strongest, healthiest donor plants for a crop of vigorous cuttings.

Also, since some plant species can produce plants that are either male or female, cloning allows the gardener to select for female-only gardens—helpful when producing flowers and fruit, without having to sort through seedlings to pick only female sprouts. Using clones is also generally faster than growing from seed.

LED grow lights are fantastic for seedlings/clones. Their compact size and ease of use can turn almost any small space into a seedling/clone garden. Even when LED grow lights were first introduced years ago, it was clear that LEDs produced strong, bushy roots on clones and strong seed starts. Early studies indicate that the higher blue-to-red ratio LED grow lights produce causes cuttings to root faster than with other lights. This is an area that needs considerably more research.

 Sloper Says

Leave your clones alone once you have taken them. Many people like to handle them, move them, and pick them up, but it's not helpful. Keep them moist and leave them alone.

Seedlings/clones don't need nearly as much light as plants in vegetative or flowering stages. In fact, too much light will stunt or kill them by pushing too much photosynthesis—the little seedlings/cuttings simply can't keep up. They rely on the stored sugars in their stems and leaves, or in the seed itself, for the energy to produce roots—diverting this energy to defend against too much light will cause rooting to slow or stop, and the seedling/ clone, to die.

Since clones don't have roots at the start, their primary method to absorb water is through their leaves, which makes them fragile. Many gardeners use humidity domes over their cutting trays to keep the moisture levels up and make it easier for cuttings to absorb moisture. A humidity dome is critical for some plants but not for others. Experiment to see what works best for your environment and cuttings.

Some gardeners swear that cuttings root faster if provided with continuous light—24 hours a day. Don't believe it—just like humans, plants need to "sleep." This is one of those "you might get away with it" garden practices, but in the long run, cuttings rooted under continuous light won't turn out as healthy as they would under an 18-hour photoperiod, and that can affect the performance of the plants as they mature.

Assuming you're using a humidity dome, once your cuttings have full, bushy roots, they are almost ready to move into their next stage: vegetative growth. But first they have to be "hardened off"—a process in which you slowly decrease the humidly under the dome. Clones accustomed to high humidity levels can dry out, wilt, and possibly die if the humidity is dropped to average room conditions too quickly. To harden off cuttings, lift the humidity dome and set it at an angle over the tray—carefully, so you don't crush the cuttings—for a couple of hours on the first day. This allows normal room air to penetrate the dome and reduces the humidity.

Keep a close eye on your cuttings during hardening off—many gardeners rush the process and kill many clones at this stage. Gradually increase this time for a few days adding an hour or two a day, then start leaving the humidity dome completely off for a few hours, gradually increasing this time until the cuttings are fully adjusted to normal room air conditions. At this point, the rooted cuttings are ready to move into the vegetative growth phase.

Cloning and seed-starting tips:

- Use a sharp scalpel or razor blade and make a clean cut of the shoot taken off the donor plant. If using a rooting hormone, don't dip cuttings into original container as you could contaminate the whole bottle. Place a little bit of it in a small bowl or shot glass, then dip or roll the cutting into it, exposing for 10–30 seconds before inserting it into its rooting media.
- Feed cuttings with plain water until roots appear.
- Switch to a ¼-strength "bloom" nutrient formula after roots have started to appear. The higher phosphorus level in the bloom nutrient encourages root growth and lower level of nitrogen is perfect because too much nitrogen can actually stunt new roots.
- Don't over-saturate the growing media. Too-wet grow media doesn't allow air exchange in the root zone and will cause the roots to rot. Seedlings are particularly vulnerable: if they are too wet, they will rot where the stem meets the grow media and fall over—this is called "damping off."

Vegetative Growth with LEDs

Once your cuttings are fully rooted and hardened off, they need to be transplanted into the grow media in which they will do their vegetative growth—building their stems and nodes, increase in size, and prepare for blooming. To support this growth, during the vegetative growth phase, light and CO_2 levels are increased. The plants are still tender, so watch your light height. The plants should have room to grow up toward the light, getting closer to it and thus increasing the light levels they receive on their own.

CO_2 supplementation is very effective in the vegetative cycle. By increasing the CO_2 concentration to approximately 1500 ppm (parts per million), you can shorten the length of time it takes to grow the plants to the desired height. They'll grow 20–30% faster than without supplementation, though CO_2 supplementation is not required for a great harvest. Don't worry if your setup won't allow for it. Just be sure you're correctly using ventilation to exchange the air in your room on a regular interval so that the CO_2 your plants consume is replenished from outside.

As with clones, don't be tempted to keep your lights on 24 hours a day during the vegetative phase. Whether the light cycle is 18/6 or 20/4 is your decision, but don't leave the lights on 24/0. Plants in their vegetative state need to sleep too and will be needlessly stressed without a dark period.

Flowering with LEDs

For short-day plants, once they have grown to the size you want, it's time to "flip" them to induce their flowering phase. This involves changing the photoperiod to a 12-hour-on/12-hour-off light cycle and increasing the light intensity.

Changing the light cycle will generate hormonal changes within the plants that trigger flowering. Many plants will also "stretch" during this phase, increasing their vertical height by double to quadruple. Make sure to plan accordingly and switch into flowering before your plants are too tall—after the stretch, they still need to comfortably fit inside your grow space. Depending on your growing system, you may need to transplant the plants into larger containers at this time. Remember, big roots equal big harvests.

Make sure to rigidly maintain your 12-hours-on/12-hours-off lighting schedule once you enter the flowering cycle. *Once again, no matter what, don't expose your garden to light during the dark period.* Also—very important—if daylight savings

 Sloper Says

I suggest using CO_2 a bit differently during flower than most growers. Start with CO_2 levels at 1500 ppm during the transition phase (generally the first two weeks) then decrease it to about 1000 ppm for the rest of the grow. CO_2 forms a carbonic acid when mixed with water vapor in the air. Carbonic acid has a bitter/sour taste. At 1500 ppm, not only can you taste CO_2 in the grow room air, you'll also be able to taste it in the final product.

time kicks in during the flowering phase, don't reset your timers. Wait until this grow is complete and change them then. Some flowering plants react very negatively to even subtle changes in light schedules. It's too easy to make a mistake that could cost you your entire harvest!

Keeping Mother/Donor Plants with LEDs

Keeping mother or donor plants is very similar to vegetative growth stage of plants that are intended to be flowered, with similar environmental and lighting requirements. The one major difference is the nutritional program

 Sloper Says

Keep your best plant for a mother plant, not the weakest one that you don't want to flower.

for donor plants. These plants are being grown to produce cuttings and not flowers. In order to produce the best possible clones, the mother plants need to be fed a properly designed regimen.

Overfed or improperly fed mother plants produce crummy clones, while properly fed donor plants will build up lots of stored carbohydrates (sugars), which are the energy source that cuttings taken from the plant will use for root production. Clones that don't have enough stored carbohydrates have a tougher time producing big, healthy roots. Closely watch mother-plant nitrogen levels: Too much, and the plant will have to use up its stored energy to process the nitrates. Too little, and the plant will become pale and weak. Also be sure to include enough calcium, which is required to build strong cell walls.

	Cloning/Seed Starting	Vegging	Flowering	Mother/ Donor Plants
Light Intensity	Low	Medium	High	Medium
Temperatures Day Night	80–80°F 70–75°	75–85° 70–75°	75–85° 70–75°	75–85° 70–75°
Humidity	50–90%	30–60%	30–60%	30–60%
CO_2 Concentration (ppm)	380 (air)–1000	380–1500	380–1000	380–1500
Light Cycle	18 on/6 off Never >20 on	18 on/6 off Never >20 on	12 on/12 off	18 on/6 off Never >20 on

Table: Optimal Garden Conditions for Plant Growth Stages

7: Grow Spaces

So now you know just about everything you need to about LEDs and LED grow lights, you've learned about optimum growing conditions, and you've decided to use an LED grow light to garden indoors. It's time to put the technical and industry stuff behind you and focus on creating a thriving indoor garden—one that produces the highest-quality crop you can muster.

Plan

What first? Make a plan, make a plan, make a plan. Your plan should include these things, at a minimum:

- A budget.
- A physical drawing of your grow space, both from above (for laying out the physical placement of items within the space) and from the side (to check that the equipment you're using will fit in the vertical height of the space).

- A list of items you need to buy, including the specific sizes of various items of equipment, such as your grow trays, light(s), fans, etc. with estimated prices.

Budget

Before you begin to build or reconfigure an LED grow room, you must have a budget. There's a lot of equipment to buy, and if you need to make any physical changes to your home, those could be costly. Figuring out a good starting point for your budget can be tricky—grow spaces can cost from hundreds to thousands of dollars, depending on equipment and configuration.

Depending on the type of grow space planned, the minimum budget for a new indoor LED garden should be at least $1,500–$2,000. This assumes you're growing light-intensive crops in a small closet-sized space. This budget should allow for the purchase of one high-quality LED light, ven-

 Sloper Says

Based on my experience working with new indoor gardeners in my hydroponics shop, it's likely that you will have to make changes during your first run, so don't spend all of your money up front.

tilation equipment, controllers/timers, and a grow system for the plants. The rest of this chapter will help you decide what equipment you need. Armed with this information, take some time to research average prices for the products you desire at your local indoor gardening centers or online. Don't forget to add in any applicable local sales tax, which can be as high as 10%, plus shipping if you're buying products from online retailers.

Once you've reached a tentative budget for your grow space, add 20% to 25% to account for forgotten details (such as fittings, tubing, and chains) as well as changes you may have to make once you're dealing in real, three-dimensional space. It's just about guaranteed that you will have to make changes, potentially lots of them if you didn't do enough homework, so it's best to account for this in your budget. Different nutrients, a quieter fan, additional controllers, and other unexpected needs always seem to crop up when lighting up a new grow space—even if you're an experienced indoor gardener. These problems will typically show up after the plants begin growing, so be warned and be ready.

Garden Drawing

Drawing out the garden's design on paper, whether by hand or using a computer-aided design (CAD) program if you're a geek, will help you to discover many important things you might otherwise overlook. Number one piece of planning advice: be realistic about how much you can grow. One of the biggest mistakes new gardeners make is cramming in too many plants. Plants need enough space between them so that their leaves don't touch or minimally touch. This allows air and light to flow down into the plants and completely surround them. In nature, dominant plants tend to crowd out smaller, weaker ones, and the same is true indoors. Give your plants enough space so they can all get along and grow strong.

Also remember that the entire grow space can't be dedicated to plants. You need space for timers, fans, filters, and irrigation systems, so plan for them too.

Grow Room Options

When it comes to finding a place for your LED grow room, let your imagination wander. With LED grow lights, you can grow in so many more spaces than you can with other garden lights, because they run cooler and require less bulky companion equipment—particularly smaller filters and ventilation fans. Once your garden is up and running, you'll likely find yourself looking around your friend's homes and thinking, "Hmmm...I could grow in that space, and that space, and that space..."

The two most basic options for an indoor grow space are a prebuilt structure such as a closet or bedroom, or a temporary or freestanding space such as a grow tent or a homebuilt grow box—either a converted piece of furniture such as a wardrobe or storage cabinet or something built from scratch. Regardless of the space you choose,

Gardening Zen

When planning the location of the garden, consider the natural temperature variations within your house or apartment. In the northern hemisphere, the northern-most rooms in the house are generally a few degrees cooler than the southern parts of the home.

make sure the roof of the structure is strong. LED grow lights are heavy, as are fans and filters which are often mounted at the top of the grow space.

Closet/Whole Room

Growing in a closet or in an entire room can be the easiest way to go because the structure is already built for you. The biggest challenge to growing in these gardens is finding a secure method to hang the lights, fans, and filters. The plaster ceilings in most houses were not designed to support very much weight. Make sure that you attach your lights and other ceiling-mounted equipment to the ceiling rafters or to brackets or a frame that is connected to the rafters.

You also need to block out all unwanted light sources such windows and/or door jams, sealing them completely so there are no light leaks during your garden's dark cycle. One way to eliminate light leaks from a standard, inward-swinging door is to hang heavy, dark curtains across it on the inside that are at least a foot taller than the door and wider on both sides, and also a bit longer than needed so they bunch up on the floor. Windows should be completely covered with light-blocking material and taped all around to ensure that no light enters from their edges.

Next, add ventilation—both fresh air coming in and garden air going out. In a full room, adding air intake and exhaust vents can be tricky and lead to an unattractive result, such as installing a vent in the hallway or the closet door. Some people cut a board to fit into the window, bolt on an HVAC duct flange, and then use an air duct to run their exhaust out the window. Neither of these two options is aesthetically pleasing, and they can both tip off the location of your indoor garden (an important consideration if you're trying to keep your garden in "stealth mode").

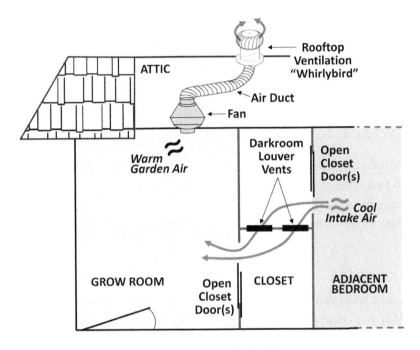

Grow Room Ventilation Idea

The most effective way to provide intake and exhaust ventilation in a whole room or built-in closet is to take advantage of adjacent air spaces. Instead of installing darkroom louver vents in a door, take a look inside the closets. A common design element in suburban American homes is a built-in closet that is essentially a big empty box between bedrooms with an interior partition, and doors on either side facing into the two rooms. If a closet in your grow room shares a wall with a closet in the next room, consider drawing cool air in from the other room through darkroom louver vents installed in the wall between the two closets. Leave the closet doors open on both sides to ensure adequate air flow, and push the clothes in the closets out of the way of the vents.

Regardless of your intake air source, it's important to exhaust the spent, heated air from your grow room out and away from your plants. If your grow room is in a one-story house or the upper floor of a multi-story home, consider cutting a hole through the ceiling of the room or closet into the home's attic space and then hanging your exhaust fan near this hole and pushing the hot air out through an air duct that extends through the attic to a rooftop ventilation "whirlybird." If your home already has an active attic exhaust system, you may be able to get away with simply exhausting into the attic.

Closet/Whole Room Pros:

- Simple, as most of the structure build out is already completed for you.
- When done right, these grow rooms can be very stealthy.
- Easy to secure by adding a lock(s).
- Easy to customize to your personal gardening style.

Cons:

- Light leaks can be tough to seal, particularly at the entrance.
- May not be worth the physical modifications if living in rented or temporary housing.

Grow Tents

Grow tents grows are perfect for temporary gardens or renters. They are available in many different sizes and shapes and can be set up and taken down quickly. There are many high-quality grow tents available as well as cheap knockoffs—be warned.

Before buying any tent, go see one for yourself at a local indoor gardening center. Does it look solidly constructed? Give it a shake test—how does it feel? Make sure the roof is capable of holding lots of weight or can be easily reinforced to hold more weight. Cheaper grow tents sometimes skimp on upper crossbeams, which limits the amount of weight they will support, while some premium models have snap-in reinforcements strong enough to hold a heavy carbon filter and a fan. Some tent manufacturers also offer snap-in equipment panels, handy for keeping timers, controllers, and fans in easy reach and protected from fluid leaks by being raised off the floor.

Heavy-duty zippers are a must as they will be opened and closed often. Most grow tents also feature gussets near the top and bottom for ventilation ducts and for electrical cords that run into and out of the tent. Make sure any tent you're considering has at least one of these gussets at both top and bottom and that you can completely close them to prevent light leaks.

⚠ Safety First

Some of the early grow tents were manufactured with PVC sheeting. When PVC heats up, it releases dioxin, which is toxic to plants and humans. Some of these early grow tents actually poisoned the gardens they were supposed to protect. PVC has been phased out of most grow tents; make sure to check before buying.

Speaking of light leaks, before you buy a tent, stand inside it and ask the shop clerk to completely close the tent and seal all of its openings. Look to see whether any light leaks into the inside—most grow tents are not completely light tight. If the tent leaks light, you may need to set it up in a room stays dark during your garden's dark period.

Some grow tents feature Velcro-closed observation windows so you can take a peek inside without disturbing the garden's environment. These can be handy for quick garden checks—as long as the observation windows do not cause light leaks and you don't open them during the garden's dark period.

Grow Tent Pros:

- Easy to set up—holes, flaps, and gussets in the correct places.
- Strong frames to hang light, fans, etc.

- Designed specifically by gardeners for gardeners.
- Extremely portable and reusable.

Cons:

- Similar-sized intake and exhaust fans are needed or they will suck the walls inward.
- May not be completely lightproof; may need to use in a darkened room.

Grow Box

A grow box is a portable grow space that can be moved—either as a self-contained unit with wheels or as an enclosure that can be disassembled and reassembled. Grow boxes differ from grow tents as they are solid structures, can be secured with locks, and can be made to be "stealthy." Many grow boxes are homemade, and there are also several companies building grow boxes ranging in size from a countertop appliance to full-sized shipping containers.

 **Sloper Says**

Note of caution: building grow boxes can be addictive. Build one and more will follow!

Homebuilt grow boxes are the most fun of all indoor grow spaces. They can be 100% custom-built; your imagination, skills, and tools are your only limits. Homebuilt grow boxes can be created in any shape or size your situation allows.

Almost anything can be converted into a grow box. The smallest of gardens can grow inside a desktop computer case, while large gardens can occupy a wardrobe cabinet or armoire. Old refrigerators and storage cabinets can be converted to gardens—assuming you have the skills and the patience to complete the conversion (including properly handling and disposing of toxic substances you might encounter, such as refrigerant).

Need a quick grow box? Foam insulation board, aka "foam core," plus good old-fashioned duct tape could be your answer. Foam core is sold in home and hardware stores in 4'x8' sheets in several thicknesses. Tape four walls together, tape on a ceiling, and cut in a door and vents, and you've got an enclosure. Buy or build a stand from 2x4s to hang your light, fan, and filter, and you're ready to grow. Foam core grow boxes are a great temporary solution and can be quickly cut down and stuffed into trash bags when not needed any more.

Grow Box Pros:

- You can build a grow space and environment that is custom-tailored to exactly meet your needs, growing style, and constraints.
- You can get very clever in configuring your garden, particularly the locations of the air vent and the electrical connections.
- They are so much fun to build—you get to build the better mousetrap.
- Your garden will recognize and reward your effort.

Cons:

- They can require lots of tools.
- They are noisy and dusty to build.
- They are time consuming to build.

Lighting

After your enclosure, the most important thing about any indoor garden is the light. After all, it's what allows us to garden without the sun. Below are a few tips regarding how to use your light most effectively.

Light Height

How high should you hang your grow light? With today's high-powered LED grow lights, internodal distances can shrink to almost nothing, which can frustrate new LED gardeners: hang the light too close and you'll have short, "squatty" plants. Hang it too high and your plants can become lanky and spindly.

Start with your LED grow light manufacturer's suggestion for light placement, then watch your garden and learn. With some experience (you know, that thing that comes just after you need it!) you'll be able to tightly control the height of your garden by raising and lowering the light. Soon, you'll be able to control the shape and height of your plants like never before and produce a lush, even canopy, without using poisonous plant growth regulators such as paclobutryzol.

Light Leaks

For a garden that contains light-sensitive plants, you must ensure that your grow room is 100% light tight. Press-on foam weather stripping works well to lightproof garden doors; choose low-density foam, as it compresses well and does not add very much resistance to closing the door.

When installing air intake vents, make sure they don't allow light to enter the garden along with air. Strategies to overcome this potential light source include:

- Making PVC light traps. These consist of at least two 90-degree PVC elbows twisted together; light can't travel around that many square corners.
- Using darkroom louver vents. Darkroom louver vents can be purchased at photography supply companies.

If you build your own light traps, paint the inside matte black, as this will reduce the amount of light that reflects inside the trap and will help to keep light contained within the trap.

Perforated Angle Iron

Anyone who has been growing indoors for a while has been there: looking up, drill in hand, swearing this will be the last time they move their grow light—this time it will finally be in the perfect spot. There is a better solution: perforated angle iron. Available at most home improvement centers, perforated angle iron is a long piece of metal bent to a 90-degree angle, with holes every inch or so. Attach lengths of perforated angle iron in the ceiling of your grow room, or on both walls near the ceiling, with appropriate mounting screws/anchors to hold the weight of your light(s). Then when you're trying out different light configurations, you can just hang the lights from the predrilled holes using cables and clips instead of drilling new holes and installing new hooks and anchors for every lighting change.

Light Movers

Light movers multiply your grow light's effective "reach" into your garden. Think about it for a moment: does the sun suddenly turn on directly overhead in the morning? Does it turn off exactly in the same position at night?

In nature, the sun rises in the east and sets in the west, but in our gardens, the "sun" turns on directly overhead and at full intensity. The sun's natural daily course across the sky provides outdoor plants with morning and evening side lighting as well as high-noon direct top lighting. When your grow light moves across the garden on a light mover, the light can reach all the plants' leaves and stems instead of just the leaves on top. It does not take too much movement to create this effect—moving the light as little as a few inches can significantly increase the amount of light that effectively reaches your plants, which will increase yields.

Design Considerations

Regardless of the size of the garden, there are many design considerations that should be made to make your life easier. From securing your garden to power placement, there is much to consider.

Access

Regardless of the type of grow space you select, make sure you can reach all of the plants in your garden. This might sound silly, but consider the depth of the space you're considering versus the length of your arm. You can't tend to your plants if you can't get to them. Installing a grow box or grow tent with a back door or side access doors can allow you to extend the area occupied by plants all the way to the edges, increasing productive space without increasing grow space size. A one-sided grow space such as a bedroom closet should not be deeper than three feet, unless you plan to grow longer arms!

Power Placement

Power management is an important design consideration for any grow space. How much electrical power do you need? How many outlets do you need? Where should they be positioned? Can you move them if necessary?

Start your power plan by computing the total amount of electricity you'll need for your garden. For each electrical device you're planning to use, such as fans, pumps, timers, and so forth, look up the power requirements, which may be listed on the device's label, in the manufacturer's documentation, or online.

If you can't locate the power requirements for a device, use a "Kill-A-Watt" meter to measure the device's electrical demand. Even if you can find a device's power consumption, it's a good idea to confirm the actual wattage with a meter. Kill-A-Watt meters are inexpensive, and by using one you'll learn quite a bit about your actual power usage—some of it might surprise you.

For example, a Kill-a-Watt will show you that most devices use a more electricity when starting and then fall to their normal usage after completely turning on. You need to plan your electrical system around the device's high electrical demand value, not its lowest. Consider what happens in the event of a power outage. When the power comes back on, all the devices will turn on at the same time, drawing their highest electrical consumption, all at the same time—which might be enough to trip a breaker and turn everything off.

When planning your garden's electrical system:

- Run upper and lower plug strips in small grow spaces to ensure short, clean electrical runs. Nothing is worse than fighting cords when trying to fix something.

 Expert Corner

Remember the 80% load rule: never exceed 80% capacity of any electrical circuit.

How do you know whether you're overloading an electrical circuit? Use V = I*R, which states: voltage (V, measured in volts) equals impedance (I, measured in amps) times resistance (R, measured in watts).

V (volts) = I (amps) x R (watts)

Electrical circuits are wired to support a certain number of amps, usually 15 or 20. Add up the amps consumed by the equipment you plan to plug into each circuit that serves your grow space.

For example, if your LED grow light uses 260 watts of 120-volt power, how many amps is it using? We need to rearrange the above equation to be like this:

I (amps) = R (watts)/V (volts)

I (amps) = 260/120

Current draw for this light = 2.16 amps

If the anticipated load on any circuit is 80% or more of its rated capacity, some of the equipment must be moved to another circuit. Overloaded circuits generate excess heat and can start fires.

- Verify the capacity and voltage of the outlets in the room. Are they 120V or 240V? 15- or 20-amp circuits? A simple way to do this is to head out to the circuit breaker panel and find the circuit that runs into the grow space. This can be accomplished easily with the aid of a "circuit tracer." The amperage is noted on the individual breaker for that electrical circuit. 120 versus 240 volts should be obvious based on the plug type in the wall. The standard two-vertical-slot outlet is 120 volts. 240-volt outlets come in a lot of varieties, are often round, and generally include at least one diagonally positioned slot. If you're not comfortable doing this kind of investigation, call an electrician. He or she can tell you what you need to know.
- Never load a circuit with equipment that draws more than 80% of its amp rating.

120V versus 240V

The difference between 120 volts and 240 volts often confuses people. From an electrical rate standpoint, the cost is the same—2.5 amps of 120 volts is the same cost as 1.25 amps of 240 volts. All residential power in North America is provided to your electric panel as 240 volts. The wiring consists of two "hot" 120-volt "legs" and a neutral "leg." For a 120-volt circuit, one of the hot legs and the neutral are used. For a 240-volt circuit, both the hot legs and the neutral are used. So what's the difference? The amperage. 240-volt devices use half the amperage as 120 volt ones.

Remember from before that watts/volts = amps
300 watts/120 volts = 2.5 amps
300 watts/240 volts = 1.25 amps

Because 240-volt devices use lower amperage, they tend to operate cooler, and you can put more of them on a single circuit. Lower operating temps don't provide much value for LED gardeners—the lights don't emit as much heat as HIDs. For commercial gardeners who use a lot of 1000-watt ballasts, however, the heat savings can add up quickly.

Cheap Timers and Controllers

Be warned: there are lots of cheaply built timers and controllers on the market, and these can create safety hazards. As with garden lights, there are plenty of manufacturers that make cheap knockoff copies of the leading garden controllers. Many of these products have not been safety tested and are imported from places where stringent safety regulations don't exist. You trust these controllers to maintain your garden's environment; don't cheap out and buy a substandard unit. Make sure any timer or environmental controller used in your garden comes from a reputable manufacturer and has a UL, CE, or ETL mark to ensure that it has been certified by a recognized testing agency.

Even the minor failure of a timer or controller, such as it keeping inaccurate time or the failure of one of its functions, can reduce your next harvest by creating out-of-spec conditions in your garden. A major failure such as an electrical short could cause a fire or a dangerous accumulation of CO_2.

 Sloper Says

If your timers or environmental controllers have user-changeable fuses, make sure to check them after every grow cycle and replace them yearly. I once had a controller fail and almost wipe out my garden over a 25☐ fuse.

Keep away from junk—it costs you even more down the road when you have to replace it.

Care for Your Extension Cords

Extension cords need to be properly managed in order to be used safely in your garden. Did you know that dozens of US homes burn down each year due to extension cords that overheated because they were left in a tightly coiled pile?

A pile or coil of powered electrical cord generates heat as the electricity spins around and around inside it. The cord can get hot enough to catch anything combustible near it on fire. To reduce this hazard, use extension cords that are the correct length whenever possible. A visit to an electronic specialty store should yield short, one-to-two-foot extension cords handy for connecting various equipment to timers and plug strips. If an appropriate length of extension cord is not available, make sure any excess length lies flat, is out of the way, and is not bunched or tightly coiled. Consider tacking long extension cord runs to the wall to keep them straight and out of the way.

Tightly Coiled Extension Cords Start Fires

When you're not using an extension cord, make sure it's properly stored. Don't coil or fold it tightly—the kinks this creates will prevent it from laying flat on next use. Coil the cord loosely and put it away flat. Putting your unused cords away with care ensures they will perform for you in the future. Also, clearly separating unused extension cords from those in use will prevent the mistake of plugging in a piled up or coiled extension cord or disconnecting a cord that is in use by mistake.

Moving Water

Women in Africa reportedly spend 25% of their time carrying water, which is a documented source of both physical disability and economic disadvantage. Do you want to become one of them? Assuming that answer is "no," then listen up: don't allow yourself to become a slave to carrying around heavy buckets of liquid. If you value your time and your back, when designing your grow room, think through *exactly* how you are going to water and fertilize your plants.

Plan for the weight of water you'll need and how far you'll have to move it. Each gallon weighs 8.3 pounds, so it adds up quick: a full five-gallon bucket weighs more than 40 pounds. Worse, the buckets and reservoirs that we use are not ergonomically designed like weights at the gym. It's a lot harder to carry 40 pounds of water dangling at the end of one arm in a bucket, held by a flimsy metal bail, than it is to carry around a 40- or 50-pound barbell.

Regardless of how you feed your garden, from hand watering to recirculating setups, you'll have to lug both water and nutrients around. Consider these ways to lighten the load:

- If you're building a grow box or adapting a closet, give yourself enough room to maneuver by building or choosing one with larger doors versus small ones.
- Consider putting the nutrient reservoir in a separate section of the closet or grow box that's partitioned off and light-sealed, so you can change the nutrients at any time instead of waiting for the garden's light cycle.
- If you have flexibility with respect to where your garden will be located, put it as close to your water source as possible.

With respect to your water source, if you filter your garden's water, reduce carrying distance by positioning the water filter as close to where you mix your nutrients as possible. Many gardeners choose to plumb reverse-osmosis filters directly into the water supply. When permanently installing a filter, consider investing in a leak detector to prevent damage from any leaks that might arise from the additional plumbing.

Small reverse-osmosis filters can be attached to many bathroom sinks, by replacing the sink's screen or aeration fitting with a screw-in hose thread adapter. A small reverse-osmosis system can then be used in the bathroom, with clean water collected directly in nutrient-mixing buckets and waste-water draining out via the sink or bathtub. This is a great option for renters, who can't make hard modifications to their homes.

Use Drip Loops

Drip loops are a common electrical safety practice; they're nothing magical but can save you a call to the electrician. A drip loop is a deliberately created low point in the electrical cord that runs between a piece of electrical equipment and the electric socket. The low point allows any water that might accidently travel along the cord to drip off before entering the socket.

For an example, go outside and look up at where the electrical main enters your house or building. Notice how the wires dip down before rising up to enter the conduit that goes into the structure. Those are drip loops. A drip loop should be used whenever an electrical device is in or near a water source, such as the pump in a nutrient reservoir. If you can, clip the low point in the cord to the wall to ensure that it stays below the outlet. It's also a good idea to make a drip loop for your outdoor holiday lights, to prevent blowing a circuit should rainwater or dew run along the cord.

Sealed Room

Unlike outdoor gardeners, indoor gardeners have the opportunity to supplement their garden's air with CO_2. As discussed earlier, plants feed themselves by converting light, water, and CO_2 into sugars through photosynthesis.

If you're planning to supplement with CO_2, make sure your grow room can be sealed tight.

 Expert Corner

CO_2 is heavier than air, so it settles. A small fan placed on the floor can stir up the CO_2 that has settled below your plants.

Obviously, a grow tent is less desirable for a CO_2-enriched garden, since the gas would seep out of its many seams, zippers, and gussets. In grow rooms and grow boxes, use foam weather stripping and "finger caulk" to fill in small gaps. Finger caulk is a rubbery material that comes in narrow strips, does not dry, and can be rolled and formed to fit into small places. Powered air vents and backdraft dampeners are also great tools to prevent CO_2 loss.

Sealing even small leaks can save on CO_2 costs. Do everything you can to close the room's ventilation openings when the exhaust fans are not running so CO_2 can't escape through your intake or exhaust vents. It's amazing how CO_2 can find its way out of even the smallest gaps.

Intake/Exhaust Fan Sizing

There are so many supposed "rules of thumb" about how to calculate the proper intake and exhaust fan size that it can make your head spin. Most formulas call for enough ventilation to change the air in the grow space on a regular interval ranging from once every five minutes to twice a minute. While these formulas are a good start, they do not consider all of the reasons a grower needs to ventilate his or her grow space: to remove heat, control humidity, and refresh CO_2 in grow room air (if the grower is not supplementing with CO_2).

There is no exact formula for how much ventilation capacity your garden needs that makes much sense in the real world every time. Every garden is different—the length of ducting runs and the number of twists and bends in the ducting will dramatically affect the ability of your exhaust fan to push (or pull) air through the system. Carbon filters add additional, and considerable, restrictive back pressure—further limiting air flow and thereby increasing required fan size.

Start by determining your grow room's size in cubic feet by multiplying the room's length x width x height. A 4-by-4-by-7-foot room, for example, contains 112 cubic feet (4 x 4 x 7). You can use this number as a starting point to select a fan—you will need one that moves at least 112 CFM (cubic feet per minute) of air. Assuming that the air ducting and filter you're using with this fan create enough backpressure to reduce effective airflow through the system by half, this fan should allow for one complete garden air exchange every two minutes.

 Expert Corner

Buy an exhaust fan that is one size larger than you think you need and then use a fan speed controller to slow it down. This lets you exercise greater control over your garden's air quality—a larger fan can always be turned down, but you can't speed up a smaller one.

If your ventilation design includes long ducting runs and bends, particularly 90-degree bends, you'll need a bigger fan to overcome increased back pressure in the system. Unfortunately, the best advice is to go up at least one size (such as from a 6-to-8-inch fan) and see what happens. When it comes to ventilation fans, bigger is generally better.

This fan sizing advice assumes you're using fans that can handle back pressure and that you're bringing enough air into the garden through vents. Inline fans can move lots of air with minimum wall watts consumed and are tolerant of moderate back pressure. Inline fans for indoor gardening come in sizes starting at 4 inches and going up to 16-inch-plus fans that look like small jet engines. If you're unsure what type of size fan to use, a local hydroponics store should be able to help you correctly size your intake and exhaust fans.

Also consider whether your design allows enough air to *enter* the grow space: drawing lots of air out of the garden without replacing that air through adequate intake vents can also increase back pressure on the system and reduce fan efficiency. Darkroom louver vents are great for air intake but are restrictive, so make sure to size them correctly—here again, bigger rather than smaller will help to ensure there is enough air coming into the room. If unsure what size louver vent to use, contact the manufacturer to help purchase the correct size based on your airflow needs.

If you can't install passive air intake vents, or if you still need more incoming air after you've installed as many intake vents as you can, you'll need to force replacement air into the grow space with an air intake fan—but don't overdo it. If your intake fan is more powerful than your exhaust fan, you may wind up forcing your garden's air out though the cracks in the room instead of through the filter. That could be a problem if you're trying to contain garden smells—some crops and fertilizers smell strongly, and you don't want to "skunk" your home or neighborhood with unpleasant smells.

 **Expert Corner**

No matter how big your intake and exhaust fans, they only cool the garden room down to something close to the temperature of the intake air. Below that, you'll need air conditioning.

The ideal ventilation setup has a slight amount of back pressure causing a negative pressure environment in the grow room—slightly less air entering than being pushed out. This will ensure that all of the air and smells travel through the filter on the way out. You'll know you have it right when there is a little resistance to opening the grow room door. If the door is difficult to open due to the exhaust fan running, that's a signal of inadequate "makeup" air.

Security

Securing your garden is essential, and that means a locked entrance. Not only does a locked door prevent someone from unintentionally breaking the dark cycle by opening the door at the wrong time, it also keeps unwanted visitors from contaminating your garden, inadvertently messing with temperature and humidity levels, or letting the CO_2 out (if you're enriching with CO_2). You're trying to emulate Mother Nature in your grow space, which is hard enough to do without the door swinging open all the time and upsetting the delicate balance that you work so hard to maintain.

 **Gardening Zen**

Did you know that many garden pests hitchhike on gardeners' clothes, shoes, or hands? Keeping visitors out of the garden helps to keep pest in check, as does washing your hands, wearing clean clothes, and changing shoes (if entering a walk-in grow space).

Your garden is *not* a souvenir to be shown off to visitors. It's where you cultivate living plants for your nutrition, enjoyment, and well-being. With respect to visitors in your garden, your position should be KEEP OUT.

8: Grow Systems

Once you've decided on the type grow room you'll use, the next big decision is which growing system you'll use. There are lots of choices: hydroponic, aeroponic, active, passive, recirculating, run to waste...If you ask five gardeners which growing system is best, you're likely to get seven to ten answers. When choosing a growing system, go with what works for you and not what is "supposed" to be the best according to some "expert." If you're just starting to garden indoors, read this chapter carefully then review the growing systems comparison chart at the end before plunking down your hard-earned cash for a growing system.

Every growing system has its pros and cons that present tradeoffs all gardeners must resolve for themselves. Some systems are easy to set up and take down but hard to clean or use lots of nutrients. Some systems require electrical power. Some systems use media that can be cleaned and reused instead of thrown out at the end of a run, which may be important for apartment dwellers with limited trash-disposal capacity.

Talk to other gardeners about their experiences with different growing systems, if you can. Whatever system you choose, stick with it for several harvests until you fully understand how it works and how to "dial it in" for your particular growing style. In your quest to become Mother Nature, lots of things get thrown at you in the beginning. Take your time and learn. If you make changes too fast, you might miss what you should be learning about gardening instead of just learning how to manage a gardening system.

Growing System Elements

Growing systems are classified by how the nutrient solution is fed to the plants. Some systems use the solution only once; these are called "run to waste" systems. Others reuse the solution for multiple feedings; these are called "recirculating" systems. Run-to-waste and recirculating growing systems can be "active" or "passive": active systems use electricity; passive systems do not.

Active versus Passive

The main difference between active and passive growing systems is that active systems need electricity to power water pumps that deliver the nutrient solution to the plants through drip lines, sprayers, trays, or channels. Passive systems don't require electricity, relying on capillary action and/or gravity to deliver the nutrient solution.

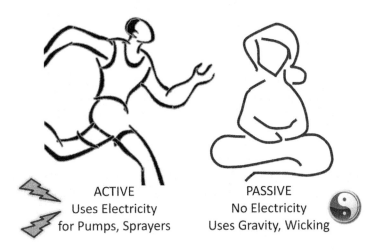

Active vs. Passive Growing Systems

Often gardeners prefer passive systems, as there is no pump to fail or stop due to a power outage. All they have to do is make sure the system is set up properly and the nutrient reservoir is filled up. "Wicking systems" passively feed the garden by capillary action: the nutrient solution moves along a cloth or rope "wick" that runs from the reservoir to the plants keeping the growing media moist. Gravity-fed systems position the reservoir above the plants, with tubing to carry the nutrient solution down to the plants.

Run to Waste

"Run to waste," a watering/feeding method in which nutrient solution is used once then discarded, is a popular gardening method for both hobby gardeners and commercial farms. Hand watering a houseplant or an outdoor plant grown in soil is the most basic form of run-to-waste irrigation. Greenhouse tomato producers often run to waste: their tomatoes are grown on the ground in pots or grow bags and watered from the top, with excess nutrients running directly into the ground. Run-to-waste watering can be used with just about any grow media.

The "waste" nutrients can be removed from the garden in many ways, including catching them in a plastic tray under a pot, a second "catch" reservoir, or even a drain hose running out of the grow space. Be sure to responsibly dispose of your waste nutrients when using the run-to-waste method. Feed the nutrient runoff to the bushes in your backyard, or dilute and spray it onto your lawn: this solution contains high-quality, bioavailable nutrients that the plants around you would eat like Easter candy. Don't toss waste nutrients down the drain if there is any alternative; see the "Salt Neutral" section later in the book for more details on why this is a poor practice.

Recirculating

Recirculating systems pump the nutrient solution from a reservoir to the plants and then collect the runoff back into the reservoir to be fed to the plants again. These systems are extremely popular with indoor gardeners because they contain the runoff and are only drained periodically—great for indoor setups where drainage may not be readily available.

Recirculating systems are typically used with hydroponic growing media, with the nutrient solution being used for a week before being changed out for fresh solution. As with run-to-waste systems, when disposing of the nutrient solution from a recirculating system, consider using it on an outside garden instead of dumping it down the drain.

Growing System Types

With these three growing system design elements in mind, let's explore the most common types of growing systems.

Ebb and Flow

Ebb-and-flow systems, also known as "flood and drain," periodically immerse plant roots in nutrient solution by pumping the solution either into a shallow tray in which the plants sit, or into individual plant grow sites. Tray-style ebb-and-flow systems consist of a formed plastic or fiberglass tray plus a reservoir, usually positioned beneath the tray. Plants are generally grown in rockwool cubes in this type of growing system.

When it's time to feed the plants, a water pump in the reservoir is turned on (usually by a timer) and pumps the nutrient solution up into to tray through an inlet tube connected to the tray at its lowest point. The tray fills up to a defined depth, determined by a second pipe called the "overflow tube" that's a few inches taller than the inlet pipe. When the solution's depth exceeds the height of the overflow tube, the solution flows back down into the reservoir through the overflow tube, thus maintaining a constant depth in the tray. The pump stays on for a set number of minutes to allow the solution to fill the grow tray and fully saturate the growing media. Then the pump is turned off, and the nutrient solution drains back into the reservoir though the pump. As the nutrient solution drains down from the tray, it also pulls air down into the plants' root zones and provides oxygen to the roots. A simple household timer or an elaborate environmental controller can be used to control the flood cycle.

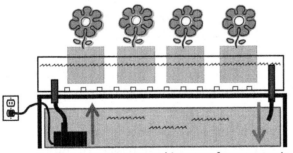

2. Tray fills to overflow tube depth, pump stays on to maintain solution depth.

1. Nutrients are pumped into tray from reservoir.
3. When pump shuts off, nutrients drain back into reservoir through pump.

Ebb and Flow Growing System

A barrel-and-bucket ebb-and-flow system operates similarly but uses a large barrel for the reservoir and individual grow buckets instead of a tray. A controller unit stands in between the barrel and the buckets and controls both the depth of the nutrient solution flood and its timing. They can be configured in just about any size and shape to fit your growing needs, and more grow pots can be added at any time, up to the capacity of the reservoir barrel.

At the start of the feed, the controller activates a pump in the reservoir cycle that starts filling the controller unit to a specified depth. Since the grow pots are all plumbed to the controller unit and since water "seeks its own level," the liquid level in all of the pots will even out to the level in the controller unit. When the pots are full, the reservoir pump is turned off and the nutrient solution is left to stand in the buckets for a few minutes. At the end of the feed cycle, a pump in the controller unit pumps all of the water back into the reservoir. Then the controller unit waits for the next feed cycle.

Grow buckets in this type of growing system consist of two plastic pots nested inside each other. The grow media and plant sit in the up-per pot, which has holes in the bottom to allow the nutrient solution to saturate the media and root zone. The lower pot is plumbed to the controller. Two-part buckets allow the gardener to rotate the plants by moving the upper pots around to even out light exposure, though this should be done infrequently and carefully to avoid damaging the plants.

One of the big advantages of ebb-and-flow growing systems is that they are extremely reliable: Each pump is on for a few minutes per cycle so your exposure to pump failure is small. There is one way to eliminate this risk altogether: as long as the gardener has a few minutes every day to manually feed the garden, a high/low bucket system can replace the pump with grav-ity and some heavy lifting.

For the high/low-bucket method, the nutrient solution is mixed in a bucket (five gallons or less, unless you want to hurt your back) that has a hole drilled near the bottom with a flexible hose attached. When it's time to feed the plants, the flexible hose is connected to the drain hole of an ebb-and-flow tray, then the bucket is hung or set above the level of the tray. Gravity will drain the nutrient solution into the tray. The bucket stays in this position for a few minutes to allow the nutrient solution to saturate the growing media, then the bucket is set down onto the floor so that the nutrient solution can drain back into it. This cycle is repeated as necessary depending on plant size and grow media type.

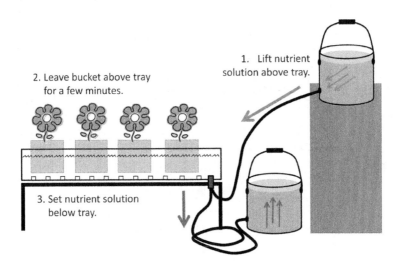

Manual High/Low Bucket Ebb and Flow Growing System

Ebb-and-Flow Pros:

- Easy to set up and move plants.
- Extremely reliable: no thin drip lines to clog.
- Forces an "air exchange" in the root zone when nutrient levels rise and fall.

Cons:

- Uses more nutrients than other systems.
- A larger pump may be needed than for other growing systems.

Drip

Drip systems are very similar to ebb and flow, but instead of filling the whole tray with nutrient solution, each plant is watered from the top via a drip line or drip ring. While drip systems typically collect the runoff to recirculate, they also come in run-to-waste models. Drip systems are appropriate for any type of grow media.

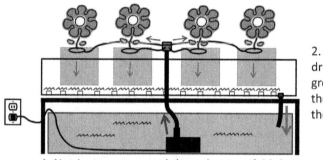

2. Nutrients drip through growing media, then drain into the tray.

1. Nutrients are pumped through a manifold that distributes the solution to plants via drip lines.

Drip Growing System

Since the nutrient solution is delivered directly to each plant, drip systems use nutrients very efficiently. They are trickier to set up: each plant needs one or more drip lines and/or drip rings, which if positioned improperly can lead to under- or over-watering. Clogged lines are also a risk. A clog in an individual drip line can kill a plant if not caught in time, and a clog in the main feed line can kill the whole garden. Plus, all of those drip lines are in the way if the plants need to be rotated or separated.

Drip Pros:

- Efficient use of nutrients.
- Drip nozzle flow rates can be customized to the needs of individual plants.

Cons:

- More complex setup with one or more drip line to each plant.
- Drip lines can clog.
- Difficult to rearrange plants.

Nutrient Film Technique or "NFT"

NFT systems suspend plants in small plastic baskets called "net pots" above a channel in which a low-volume trickle of nutrient solution constantly flows across their bare roots. In the ideal NFT system, the water level is very thin, hence the name nutrient "film." The plants' roots grow into a thick mat in the channel, with the bottom of the mat laying in the nutrient film and the top moist but exposed to air. NFT systems, properly used, provide an optimal balance of water, nutrients, and oxygen to the plants, accelerating growth and promoting heavy harvests.

Because NFT systems do not use growing media such as soil or rockwool, they are highly sensitive to interruptions. Growing media provides a great buffer for plants: it keeps roots moist between feedings, can absorb and release nutrients when the plant needs them, and retains oxygen in the root zone. Without growing media to protect them, NFT-grown plants can quickly dry out if the film is interrupted for any reason—a power outage, failed pump, or clogged line can kill an NFT garden in less than a day if not discovered right away. Consider using an uninterrupted power supply (UPS) if you live in an area where blackouts are common.

2. Nutrients flow across bare roots of plants.

3. Solution drains into reservoir.

1. Nutrient solution continuously pumped up into NFT channel from reservoir.

Nutrient Film Technique Growing System

NFT Pros:

- Superior plan growth due to high oxygen levels.
- No grow media expense.
- Efficient use of nutrients.

Cons:

- Crop fails quickly if the pump fails.
- You need to have a replacement pump on hand and check your garden frequently.

Aeroponics or "Aero"

Similar to NFT, aeroponics is a growing method that exposes the bare roots of plants to air and to nutrient solution. In this case, the roots hang in a chamber in which nutrient solution is either sprayed directly onto the roots or misted into the air surrounding the roots.

Aeroponics was developed in the 1940s as a method to study plant root development. Aero differs from NFT in that the roots are contained with a large area versus a channel, and they are not necessarily constantly exposed to the nutrient solution. The plants consume nutrients from solution droplets that land on their roots, and the humid environment in the root chamber prevents the roots from drying out.

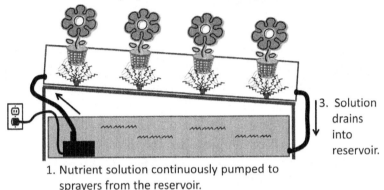

2. Nutrients sprayed onto bare roots of plants.

3. Solution drains into reservoir.

1. Nutrient solution continuously pumped to sprayers from the reservoir.

Aeroponic Growing System

Many commercially produced cloning machines use aeroponic techniques to root cuttings. Aero systems are also available for full-sized plants, though they command a smaller share of the market than other types of growing systems. This is because, like NFT, aeroponic systems are more susceptible to failure—a power outage or pump failure can instantly leave the garden high and dry. Consider using an uninterrupted power supply (UPS), if you live in an area where blackouts are common.

Aeroponic Pros:

- Superior plant growth due to high oxygen levels.
- No grow media expense.
- Efficient use of nutrients.

Cons:

- Crop fails quickly if the pump fails.
- You need to have a replacement pump on hand and check your garden frequently.

Deep Water Culture or "DWC"

DWC is a growing method in which the plants' bare roots are immersed in a solution of highly oxygenated, nutrient-rich water. The plants are suspended in the solution using plastic net pots or something similar depending on the manufacturer. Air is pumped into the DWC reservoir though air pumps and stones, earning this technique the alternate moniker "bubbleponics." DWC systems are often homemade setups that include a five-gallon bucket, a bucket lid with attached net pot, an air pump, and an air stone. Commercially produced systems are available in a large variety of configurations.

Deep-water culture is a misnomer since the nutrient solution can actually be shallow or deep in these systems. "Direct water culture" would be better, since the root zone is completely immersed in the nutrient solution.

Plants are suspended in a nutrient solution reservoir that is constantly aerated with an air pump and stone.

Deep Water Culture Growing System

DWC systems are simple to set up and operate. Systems that use individual buckets allow plants to easily be rotated or moved to take best advantage of available light. DWC's downside is the risk of pump failure: if the air pump fails and the bubbles stop, the plant(s) can drown in a matter of hours. Garden checks are required several times a day.

Like NFT and aeroponics, power failures can kill this type of garden. Again, consider using an uninterrupted power supply (UPS) if you live in an area where blackouts are common.

DWC Pros:

- Great growth due to high oxygen levels.
- Can be inexpensively made at home.

Cons:

- Plant(s) can drown if the air pump fails.
- You need to have a replacement pump on hand.
- Frequent garden checks necessary.

Growing System Type	Electricity Required	Complexity	Fault Tolerance
Ebb and Flow - Automated	Yes	Med	Med
Ebb and Flow – High/Low Bucket	No	Low	High
Drip Irrigation	Yes	High	Med
Nutrient Film Technique (NFT)	Yes	High	Low
Aeroponic	Yes	High	Low
Deep Water Culture (DWC)	Yes	Low	Med

Table: Growing Systems Comparison

Media Considerations

Except for with the purely hydroponic growing systems (NFT, aeroponic, and DWC), you'll need to choose a growing media. There are many things to consider: simplicity, environmental friendliness, clean-liness, weight, and cation-exchange capacity. Also think about where your garden is situated and how you will dispose of used grow media. If you live upstairs, you might want to select a lightweight media such as rockwool instead of heavy grow rocks. If you want to grow in soil, where will you dispose of used soil? Recycling indoor garden soil into outdoor beds is an environmentally friendly choice so long as you screen out and dispose of any excess perlite in the mix. Perlite, a white, lightweight material made from volcanic rock, will rise to the top of the beds when watered, where it will be blown around your yard by the wind.

Cation-exchange capacity (CEC) measures how well a grow media retains or "binds" elemental minerals contained in the nutrients you feed the plants. Growing media with higher CEC will be able to feed the plants longer than media with low CEC. Naturally derived growing media, in-cluding shredded coconut husks ("coco coir") and peat have relatively high CEC, in contrast with manmade media such as rockwool cubes and grow rocks that provide little if any CEC. When using a media with high CEC, be sure to alternate feeding and watering to prevent over-fer-tilization, such as feed-water-water-feed-water-water. Then watch the plants carefully to look for signs of over- or under-feeding, and adjust accordingly.

It's not always obvious whether a particular growing media has a high or low cation exchange capacity. Indoor potting mixes can look like soil but may not have high enough CEC to maintain nutrition. If you're not 100% certain about the CEC value of a grow media, ask your garden retailer for details. Pick one media to start with, and stick with it for your first few harvests. Remember: in the beginning, gardening is all about learning, so go slow with changes. The table below will help you choose from the most common growing media. If you're new to growing indoors, start out with a high-quality soil or rockwool.

Media Type	Pros	Cons	Cation Exchange Capacity
Soil Mixes	Readily available, usable out of the bag, can be pre-charged with nutrients, forgiving, good for beneficial microorganisms	Heavy to carry, can be over watered, messy	Low to High
Coco Coir	Reusable, environmentally friendly, great for beneficial organisms, usable out of the bag	Heavy to carry, messy	Medium
Rockwool	Simple to use, lightweight	Not environmentally friendly, needs conditioning	None
Expanded Clay Pellets (aka Hydroton, Grow Rocks)	Great aeration, reusable	Heavy to carry, messy, needs to be prewashed	Little to None
Perlite	Lightweight, great for "lightening" up soil/soilless mixes	Messy, dust is an inhalation hazard	None

Table: Pros and Cons of Popular Growing Media

Growing System Gotchas

While setting up most growing systems is relatively simple, it's easy to get crossed up by one of these common goofs.

Kinked Tubing

Kinked hoses can spell disaster for an indoor garden. It's surprising how even a small bend in a hose can cause it to all but shut off flow. When it comes to tubing, like all critical equipment, "when in doubt, throw it out."

If the tubing that comes with a new growing system is kinked or if your tubing becomes kinked from poor storage or misuse, *replace it*. Don't be penny-wise and pound-foolish; tubing is cheap, and your garden is a labor of love.

Also, remember that "haste makes waste." If your growing system includes tubing, just assume it's kinked, and check it every chance you get. Be vigilant looking for telltale signs—drooping plants and light, dried-out containers. Whatever you do, don't let kinked tubing be your garden's downfall.

 Sloper Says

I have a friend who was working on her garden just prior to going on vacation. Late for a flight, she quickly dropped the pump for her ebb-and-flow system into the reservoir without checking to be sure the hose was straight. When she got home, she found the garden completely dried and fried: the tube that irrigated her tray had a pinch in it when it was purchased, creating a weak point that twisted just enough to almost completely block nutrient flow through the line. Fifty cents worth of new tubing when the system was set up, and/or a 10-second check when the pump was placed in the reservoir, would have saved the garden.

Leak Detector

Adding a leak detector to your garden equipment just in case something becomes backed up or spills is a good idea. It's easy to have a leak in your garden—with all of the hoses, fittings, reservoirs, and trays; it's inevitable that something will leak over time. Leak detectors range from simple units that sound an audible alarm to wireless sensors that call, text, or Tweet to alert you of the flood.

Also keep a wet/dry vacuum nearby just in case. If you don't already have one, consider buying one of the vacuum heads designed to sit on a five-gallon bucket that started showing up in hardware stores recently. They're inexpensive, and they're small enough to fit in all but the smallest of indoor gardens.

Odor Control

Let's face it: sometimes plant nutrients and the plants themselves stink. Good odor control can keep you on the good side of family and neighbors. Most indoor gardeners want a garden that does not interfere with the household or draw attention to itself. Uncontrolled garden smells defeat both purposes. They're also an invitation for would-be intruders in your garden.

A newer tool to fight garden smells is the AC-48 carbon found in more recently introduced air filters. AC-48 is activated charcoal that has been finely ground, which provides effective air cleaning at a lower cost and with a longer useable life—using less activated carbon than its older counterpart, pelletized carbon. AC-48 filters are smaller and much lighter than their pelletized carbon equivalents, making them easy to hang up out of the way.

Speaking of filters, there's a longstanding debate about whether it's better to draw or blow air through a filter. Ask people their opinion and you'll hear both sides, with lengthy justifications on each side. Make this decision based on your ventilation setup and where you have the room to set or mount your fan and filter. The best argument for sucking though the filter is that you can use a pre-filter, which will extend the life of the filter itself.

While the fan/filter doesn't care too much about suck versus blow, the ducting does. Ducting works better when its being blown open instead of sucked through, which makes it want to close in due to back pressure.

Configure your ventilation setup so you can get to the back of both the fan and filter, in case they need service or repairs. Also make sure there are as few sharp bends in your ventilation ducting as possible. Then don't fret about it.

9. How to Feed Plants

When it comes to feeding plants, it turns out that the "how" is just as important as the "what." It takes a lot to properly feed a garden: you need to determine how much nutrient solution your garden needs, how to make the solution as available to the plants as possible, how to identify nutrient deficiencies and excesses, and when beneficial microorganisms might be helpful. We'll dig into the "what" to feed your garden in Chapter 10. In this chapter, you'll find ideas and information about the hows and whys of plant nutrition that you may have not seen or thought of before. Like this:

Feed Schedules—Don't Blindly Trust Them

Don't trust the "standard" feeding schedules printed on the back or side of bottles and boxes of nutrients designed for indoor growing. Most of these feeding charts were developed for experienced gardeners who grow heavy-feeding plants under 1000-watt HID lamps. Almost everybody else will overfeed their gardens if they use these nutrient levels.

Making matters worse, marketing campaigns for indoor garden nutrients are designed to make you believe that you need lots and lots of bottles. The companies that make and sell these products want you to think you need a multi-part base nutrient formula and a seemingly unlimited number of supplements or else your yields will suffer. They might also tell you that your yields will *explode!* if you supplement with the latest bottle of plant go-go juice. Some supplements even promise results bordering on supernatural, such as vibrationally activated water that purportedly kills or prevents mildew or a spray that restores a plant's "natural genetic photosynthetic speed" to produce heavy harvests.

 Sloper Says

Many gardeners, searching for better results, keep trying out different nutrients thinking that they will find their "holy grail"—nutrients that allow their plants to thrive trouble-free.

But while searching for that Holy Grail, what did the gardener acquire? Experience. *The health of any garden depends more on the gardener's experience than on the nutrients it was fed. With experience and your best "meter," YOUR EYES, you will soon master indoor garden nutrition.*

Stop listening to what the nutrient manufacturers say about what, how much, and how often to feed your garden, and start paying more attention to your plants. They will tell you when they want to be fed. Nutrient manufacturers are in the business of selling bottles, more bottles, and even more bottles of plant food—not tending your garden. The more bottles you buy, the more money they make.

Feeding Your Plants: How Much?

With plant nutrition, less is usually more. Plants are much more in control of what they "eat" than we give them credit for: they've developed complex systems to attract the specific minerals they need and repel the ones they don't, primarily through root secretions. These secretions, also called "root extrudates," change conditions in the root zone, such as raising or lowering pH or changing the amount of sugars in the soil, which affects the composition of beneficial microorganisms in the soil and also nutrient availability. Overfeeding can break down these regulatory processes.

All you really need to do is provide your garden with a wide range of the required nutrients, not too much and not too little, so the plants can pick and choose what they need in order to grow. Choose a good-quality nutrient designed to be used with your type of growing system, and start by feeding your plants at about half the suggested strength. Then keep a close eye on them.

Is their green color getting lighter or darker? Lighter generally means the plant needs more nitrogen and possibly magnesium. Underfed plants may also develop weak stems and branches, grow slowly, or develop mildew. Any obvious problems should be treated directly (such as staking the plant or spraying for fungus), and the feeding solution should also be strengthened a bit. Continue to monitor and adjust until you find the feeding level at which the plants are lush and vigorously growing, able to stand on their own and absorb high levels of good-quality light.

 Good Practice

When watering plants in pots or containers, make sure you're really saturating the grow media. It's easy to pour some nutrient solution over a plant, see it quickly run out the bottom, and believe the job is done. Not necessarily. The best way is to water a small amount, wait 3—4 minutes, water a bit more, wait 3—4 minutes, and then water the plant until saturated. The first two small waterings break the surface tension within the media and allow for full watering.

A plant's nutritional needs may change over its life cycle, particularly with respect to potassium, one of the "big three" nutrients— nitrogen, phosphorous, and potassium. Many plants consume potassium in higher levels during their flowering and fruiting phases, which is why "bloom boost" supplements with high potassium levels are so popular. But with that popularity comes a problem: an overdose of phosphorus. We'll talk about this in greater detail in chapter 10.

Overfeeding is worse than underfeeding, because it's harder to correct. You may be able to flush away some of the excess nutrients in a hydroponic system, but your garden might be stuck with the excess bound up in soil/soilless media. Flushing is discussed later in this chapter.

LEDs and Garden Nutrition Levels

You may have heard that nutrient levels should be lower for LED-lit gardens versus gardens with other lights. In the early days, LED gardeners did generally feed ¼- to ½-strength solutions since the older LED lights didn't have much power or produce much heat. Lower light and lower heat slows a plant's transpiration, reducing growth and lowering nutritional needs.

The newer generation of LED grow lights, with higher light output and improved light penetration, grow large plants with nutritional profiles similar to plants grown under any other indoor garden light. Ignore any advice you may find online or elsewhere about feeding LED gardens weak nutrient solutions. Plants grown under newer LED grow lights may even need *more* nutrition than their HID counterparts—it would be hard to say for sure without formal trials in a laboratory setting.

Foliar Feeding

Foliar feeding involves spraying a diluted nutrient solution directly onto the leaves. Plants can readily absorb nutrients through their leaves, just as they can though their roots. Foliar feeding is a great way to correct nutrient deficiencies or to make up nutritional

 Good Practice

Be sure to "spot test" the foliar spray on one plant to make sure spraying does not cause problems that are worse than the one you're spraying to correct...

differences between plants when you're feeding light- and heavy-feeding plants from the same reservoir.

Make sure to avoid spraying a solution that's too strong—overfeeding this way will burn the plants. Mix up a solution that's a quarter to half the strength of the nutrient solution you're feeding to the plants, then test spray one or two plants to see how they react before spraying the whole garden. If you see no result, make the spray solution a little bit stronger, and try again on a different plant. Keep testing until you find the strength that works.

pH and Nutrient Availability

The pH of the nutrient solution you feed your plants, how acidic or basic, matters somewhat—but far less than many gardeners think. A pH of 7.0 is defined as neutral: below that, solutions are acidic and above that they are basic. If your nutrient solution is way out of the normal range, either too acidic or basic, your plants will have a more difficult time absorbing the nutrients they need. Fortunately, most plants tolerate a wide range of pH values: for most indoor garden plants, a pH between the low 5s and high 6s is fine.

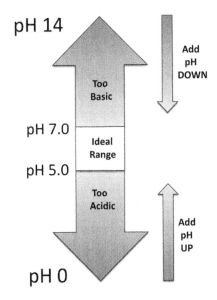

General pH Range for Plants

Adjusting the pH of your nutrients is very simple. If the pH is too low (5 or less), add pH up solution (a base). If the pH is too high, (7 or more) add pH down (an acid). Both pH up and pH down solutions are available at any hydroponics store.

Sloper Says

I once fed a soil-based crop a nutrient solution that was very acidic—pH below 4—for its entire life cycle due to a pH meter problem. I knew from looking at the garden that there was a problem, but I didn't suspect pH as the cause, because I assumed the meter was working fine. It appeared to calibrate properly. Fortunately, the crop was growing in a high-quality soil with lots of beneficial microorganisms added to the mix. The soil was able to buffer the negative effect of pH, so while this grow did not produce the best yield, it still produced a harvest.

Indoor gardeners tend to stress about pH levels, mostly because they've been trained to. Nutrient manufacturers, hydro shop staff, and indoor gardening magazines all warn indoor gardeners on a regular basis that without proper pH levels, your plants will not be able to take up the nutrients they need, and the garden will suffer. Thus, at the first sign of a problem, many rookie gardeners blame out-of-spec pH. After all, since they followed the instructions on their nutrient bottles exactly, the problem must not be their fault. It must be due to pH swings causing nutritional lockouts.

There are also growers that believe in changing the pH by 0.1 of a point a week during flowering—for example, 5.8, 5.9, 6.0, 6.1, 6.2…While these gardeners swear this practice makes a difference, fine-tuning pH to this degree is completely unnecessary. There is simply no reason to be a slave to your garden to that extreme.

Many extremely knowledgeable indoor gardeners skip the pH adjustment process ENTIRELY and have amazing results. Do your own experimenting and find what works in your garden. You just may find yourself leaving the pH meter on the shelf!

The pH should be allowed to drift up or down for both soil/soilless and hydroponic growing systems. Letting the pH drift within reason provides opportunities for all of the various minerals within the solution to be absorbed and lets the plant choose what it takes in based on its needs, instead of force-feeding it with a strict, pH-driven regimen.

Testing pH

There are three ways to check the pH of your nutrient solution: using a pH meter, litmus paper, or chemical indicator drops.

A pH meter is the easiest way to check pH. These electronic devices have a glass electrode that's paired to a digital display. Some also measure the temperature of the solution, and all have the one thing in common: you absolutely must read and follow the owner's manual. Be sure to keep pH meters cleaned and calibrated. An un-calibrated meter is useless, and a meter with nutrient solution built up on the probe will produce false readings.

- Pros: Easy to use.
- Cons: Expensive, needs regular cleaning and calibration.

Litmus paper is a simple way to measure pH. These paper strips, coated with pH-sensitive chemicals, change color when exposed to any solution. Simply tear off a piece and dunk it the nutrient solution. Wait for it to change color and then compare to the included chart to "read" the pH.

- Pros: Inexpensive.
- Cons: Must use litmus paper that measures the correct range (4.0–8.0), can be difficult to see subtle color differences, can degrade—needs to be used by expiration date.

 Good Practice

Whenever you get a "strange" or unexpectedly out-of-range pH measurement from a meter, clean and calibrate it and try again. It's also a good idea to keep litmus paper or chemical indicator drops on hand to confirm erratic readings.

Chemical pH-testing drops are similar to litmus paper as they also rely on a color change to indicate the pH of the tested solution. To use the chemical indicator drops, fill the small sample tube included with the test kit with the nutrient solution being tested, add as many testing drops as the manufacturer recommends, and shake. The solution will change color; compare the color to the included color chart to determine pH. Dispose of the solution in the test vial by rinsing it thoroughly down the drain. NEVER pour it back into your nutrient reservoir, and NEVER add the drops directly into the reservoir—period.

- Pros: Cheap.
- Cons: Can be difficult to see subtle color differences, can degrade—needs to be used by expiration date.

Safely Adjusting pH Levels

Mishandling pH up and down solutions can be dangerous—these concentrated acids and bases cause chemical burns. When working with these solutions, be careful about these things:

- Wear glasses or safety glasses when adjusting pH. Splashing pH up or down solution into your eyes is dangerous. Best case, it's painful. Worst case, you have permanent eye damage. ALWAYS use eye protection when adjusting pH.
- Know where the closest water source and shower are, in case of a really big spill. The quicker you wash off the acid or base, the better.
- Decant into manageable bottles. It does not matter how good of a pourer you are, pouring drops from a gallon bottle is never easy, especially when you're trying to be accurate. Use small bottles, preferably with flip tops, so it's easy to add lots or just a few drops. Make sure to clearly label them.
- Different manufacturers make different-strength pH up and down solutions—don't assume they are all the same. Some manufacturers pride themselves on making weak up/down as a safety precaution. Others brag about their solution being the strongest on the market because it's a better value. If the strength of the solution is not printed on the label, ask the retailer how strong the solution is, or look it up on the Internet. Regardless, when changing brands, use the new solution sparingly until you're familiar with its strength.

- If you decide to dilute an up or down solution, make sure you put the water into the bottle first and then pour in the acid/base. This is basic lab technique: if for some reason the acid/base breaks out into a reaction (unlikely, but possible), there's a small amount of acid/base in lots of water instead of a little bit of water with lots of acid/base in it to fly at you.

- For organic gardening, consider using citric acid for pH down and potassium bicarbonate for pH up.

Beneficial Organisms

Beneficial organisms, also known as "beneficials" or "bennies," include any organism that helps the plant. While this is a whole range of beings including birds, humans, and insects, generally the term bennies refer to soil-based microorganisms that provide a whole range of benefits to the host plant.

Beneficial organisms help translocate water within the grow media, colonize the roots to provide protection from invaders, and make nutrients available to the plant through moving minerals within the plant and chemically releasing "locked-up" ones. Beneficial organisms used indoors generally fall into four categories; funguses, bacteria, nematodes and specific predators.

 Safety First

Bases (pH up) feel slimy on the hands. If your hands feel slimy after handling pH up, wash them immediately with LOTS of water. Chemical burns hurt for a long time—just say no!

If you're refilling a small bottle with pH up or down and it gets warm—you've topped up with the wrong solution. When acids and bases combine, they give off heat. Safely pour the mixture out, wash your hands and the bottle and start again.

- Funguses are the heavy lifters of the indoor beneficials. It's their job to break down heavy ligneous materials: the hard stuff trees and bushes are made from, called "brown material" by composters. Funguses form a symbiotic relationship with the roots and grow tiny calciferous tubes that transport water and nutrients from the soil to the roots. The most widely used indoor fungus are mycorrhizae and trichoderma.

- Bacteria are responsible for breaking down cellulose-based materials, what composters refer to as "green waste." They are much less mobile than fungus as they depend on the presence of water film to migrate. A commonly used indoor bacteria is bacillus subtilis.
- Nematodes are commonly deployed as a cure to a problem in the garden. They are very small worm-looking creatures that are known to attack over 200 different soil-based pests. For indoor gardens, nematodes can be used to control some of the nastiest pests such as fungus nats, thrips, and leaf miners.
- Specific predators eat specific garden pests. There are hundreds of them available depending on what is invading, from aphids to mites. Examples include ladybugs, predator mites, praying mantis, and green lacewings.

The specific product used to introduce beneficial organisms to an indoor garden depends of the type of growing media used. In loose mixes, dry powder containing beneficials can be mixed in when planting clones or added when transplanting. Be careful to not smother young roots – adding too much power directly to the roots of a small clone can kill it.

In solid media, such as rockwool, beneficials can be watered in. There are specific products made for this purpose, if you're not sure about one, check with your local gardening shop or contact the product's manufacturer to make sure it should be used in this fashion.

Beneficial organisms are a very big part of the "soil food web," described by the famous and insightful garden writers Jeff Lowenfels and Wayne Lewis. They wrote an outstanding book called *Teaming with Microbes* that describes in plain language how beneficial organisms improve garden results; consider it a must-read.

Here are a few pointers to keep in mind with using beneficial organisms in your garden:

- Chlorine and chloramines in the water used for your nutrient solution will kill beneficial organisms. If you're using bennies, you must filter these compounds out of the water you use to feed your garden.
- Blackstrap molasses is a source of sugars, potassium, calcium, and sometimes iron (check the label). Adding a teaspoon to a tablespoon per gallon to your nutrient solution is a great way to feed your beneficials and add flavor to your plants. Blackstrap molasses is not recommended for use in recycling hydroponic systems.
- Read and follow manufacturer's instructions to the letter – some have specific requirements including keeping them refrigerated.

Flushing

Flushing is a process by which excess nutrients are removed from the root zone. This is only a concern when using mineral salt-based nutrients and is generally not a useful technique when using organic nutrients. Organic nutrients tend to bond to the soil particles in very complex ways that flushing rarely affects. There are two reasons to flush your plants: correcting for overfeeding, and clearing out unused nutrients at the completion of the grow.

To correct for overfeeding, wash lots of water through the growing media. Generally, you'll need to use a volume of water that's two to four times the size of the plants' growing containers to flush. For instance, if you're growing in a 3-gallon pot, flush with 6–12 gallons of plain water—no nutrients.

 Gardening Zen

If you properly feed your plants through the grow, there should be no reason to have to flush your plants either during the grow or at the end.

Flushing at the end of the grow is simpler. In recirculating systems, just use plain water for the last week's "feeding." Some gardeners like to change the reservoir partway through the last week to ensure a thorough flush. In hand watering and run to waste systems, just feed the garden plain water during the final week.

Some gardeners use flushing solutions to aid in the process. These solutions contain sugars that help to break the bonds between the plant and the minerals in the growing media. Once these bonds are broken, the minerals are freed and can be washed out of the grow media.

"Salt Neutral"

OK, so we have all heard about carbon neutral, but have you considered being salt neutral? Consider the nutrients you're using—are they mineral-salt based? How do you dispose of them? Most people dump them down the drain and don't think much about it. This is a problem, since they are not completely removed at wastewater treatment plants. Over time these salts concentrate in our lands and water supplies. It's becoming such a serious threat in commercial agriculture that in certain regions, serious remediation techniques are being applied.

Consider going salt neutral with organic nutrients. Organics have come a long way from their introduction into the indoor garden market just a few years ago. Early smell problems have been greatly reduced, and most of the newer formulations don't require pH adjustment. It's a win-win for the environment and you. Move over carbon: it's time for salt neutral to take the spotlight!

High-Quality Water

We've all heard the expression "crap in equals crap out." The quality of the water you feed to your garden matters—potentially a lot.

The concentration of "the stuff" in water is measured in parts per million or ppm for short. The higher the ppm, the greater the amount of impurities in the water. This "stuff" can bind with the nutrients in your reservoir, causing them to become locked up and unavailable to your plants. It also contributes to the strength of your nutrient solution and can make an otherwise properly mixed feed solution too strong—thus overfeeding the plants.

You need to start with good-quality water, purchased or filtered to not more than 100 ppm. As mentioned before, no matter what else you do, you must remove the chlorine and chloramines from your feed solution when growing with beneficials. Chlorine is very harmful to beneficial organisms and will reduce or eliminate their colonies.

 **Expert Corner**

From an indoor gardening perspective, water quality is measured in "parts per million" or PPM for short. This is a reading of how many ions (such as calcium, magnesium, sodium, lead, etc.) are present in the water.

A 10 PPM reading means that there are 10 ions per one million water molecules.

Before you decide on your filtration needs, test your water with a "ppm meter" available from your local hydroponics store. It's also a good idea to contact your local water management office for a water report. This will give you a good idea of the quality of your water and whether there are changes in the water supply during the year. For example, Long Beach, California uses local ground water for most of the year, but during certain times imported water is mixed into local supplies, changing the mix of water-borne elements significantly. Changes in the composition of your water supply can explain incurable pH swings or nutrient precipitation (sludge) in your reservoir.

Filtration

It's always a good idea to filter the water you use for gardening, regardless of its quality. The initial hardness (ppms) of the water will dictate the filtration strategy—reverse osmosis or carbon filtration. Reverse-osmosis filters are used when your water quality is fair to poor—more than 100 ppm of dissolved minerals. Use a carbon filter when the source water has an initial ppm reading of under 100.

Reverse osmosis (R/O) water is produced by a filter system that uses pressure to force water through a membrane that traps and rejects contaminants, which are discarded as a wastewater stream. R/O units are rated by how much wastewater to clean water they produce. Cheap units waste a lot of water, with waste-to-good ratios as high as 5:1. Efficient units can run as low as 1:1. Many of the newer systems can produce water that is very clean—down to a few ppm—though as the ratio of good water to wastewater drops closer to 1:1, R/O filters may allow more contaminants through. Contact the manufacturer to get exact performance specifications; good suppliers are happy to supply this info.

Carbon filters are a less expensive alternative to R/O systems if your water source does not have very many impurities. Carbon filters remove chlorine and chloramines, but that's about it. The best thing about these filters is that they produce no wastewater.

If you're using well water, you need to take extra care because well water can contain unknown amounts of impurities (calcium, magnesium, sodium, carbonates, sulfates, etc.), plus pathogens such as bacteria, viruses, and other microorganisms that can cause disease. While an R/O filter can remove unwanted mineral impurities, it won't filter out pathogens.

To clean up well water, use a water filter that exposes the water to ultraviolet light, particularly UV-C. UV-C is very good at killing viruses and bacteria. Run your R/O-cleaned water through a separate UV-C filter if you're using well water, or buy a combination R/O and UV-C filter setup. Most people who live on well water already have methods to filter and sterilize their water.

Alkaline versus Alkalinity

Many people get confused about the difference between alkaline and alkalinity, or think they're the same thing. They're not. Alkaline means having a pH greater than 7 (also called "basic"), while alkalinity is the concentration of ions in a substance (such as sulfates, phosphates, silicates, or carbonates), measured in ppm. The classic example comparing alkaline and alkalinity is that the pH (alkaline level) of a solution can be lowered by dissolving CO_2 into it, while the alkalinity (ppms) of the solution remains unchanged.

If you're using R/O water, consider blending in a little dechlorinated city water. The city water's alkalinity helps to buffer pH fluctuations in your nutrient solution. Most hydroponic nutrient manufacturers assume you are using water with some alkalinity. Consider 60–80 initial ppm to be a good starting point for your water blend.

Other Lab Techniques

Every serious indoor gardener should consider taking a college-level general chemistry course, *and the lab*. There is so much interesting science to learn, but more importantly, you'll learn lab techniques that improve safety, save money and time, and make your garden more successful. Some of the products we use in our gardens are expensive, and we don't want to waste them due to simple mixing and handling errors.

- Never pour back into a bottle. Period. Any bottle. Trying to save a bit by pouring any excess back into the bottle is NOT a good idea. The little amount you're saving presents a big risk of contaminating the whole bottle.
- Wash your hands before and after mixing any nutrients, just like your mother had you do before eating. This simple technique helps prevent contamination.

- Mix in the reservoir, not in the measuring cup. There is a reason hydroponic nutrient manufacturers split some formulas into multiple parts. It's because many of the compounds that are stored in separate bottles will react with compounds in the other bottles if they are exposed to each other at full strength. When they react, the minerals bind together and become unavailable to the plants, causing incomplete nutrition. When multi-part nutrient solutions are mixed into a reservoir that provides sufficient dilution, the reactions between the minerals in the various bottles are slowed or stopped altogether.

- Which bottle to start with? If you are using any of the "three part" nutrient programs, add the micronutrient solution first, then the grow and the bloom formulas, starting with the bottle that contains the highest phosphorus content. Diluting the micronutrients first helps to ensure that they are fully dissolved and won't bind up and become unavailable.

- Put tops on bottles right away. This might sound trivial, but we all have knocked over open bottles.

- Don't rinse the nutrient/pH solution cap in the nutrient reservoir. Some growers like to use the bottle top as a measuring cup. For some reason, after they measure out what they need, many of these gardeners decided to rinse the cap by swishing it in the nutrient reservoir. This is a *really* bad idea as it contaminates the rest of the bottle.

10. What to Feed Plants

There are many well-written books about plant nutrition; you should read several. This chapter isn't meant to replace any of them. Instead, it examines plant nutrition from the perspective of an amateur gardener who's looking at a nutrient bottle or box and trying to make sense of it. For each of the primary, secondary, and micronutrients, we'll discuss what the nutrient does inside a plant and how that translates into the specific types of nutrient compounds that best address these needs. Let's start at the very beginning:

How to Read a Nutrient Label

Deciphering the label on a nutrient bottle or box can be a daunting task. There are so many different formulas, many claiming explosive growth, or increased yields over their competitors. Trying to compare them side by side may not reveal much unless you know what to look for.

By state law, which of course varies state to state, nutrient manufacturers are required to include some specific information about what's contained into the product. Many other compounds are also contained in most products, but since they are not specifically required to be listed, they're not. Nutrient labeling regulations are so complicated that it's not unusual for products from reputable companies to get pulled from the market because their labels don't conform to labeling requirements in some way.

The table on the next page will come in handy while you're trying to make sense of a nutrient label. Use it as a reference when reading the rest of this chapter. It lists the elements needed by plants with their chemical forms plus common compounds that contain them.

Expert Corner

Plant nutrition does not change dramatically when converting from vegetative to flowering states. I have personally used the same formula of nutrients for both the veg and flower states.

I know plenty of commercial growers that use the same single powder-based nutrient in both grow and bloom stages without a single additive and produce excellent results. Their methods have been shown effective in everything from soil to rockwool.

Basically what I am saying is that a big bunch of the bottles in the hydroponics shops are a waste of money. Generally, learning better gardening techniques through experience is going to give you better results than buying expensive bottles.

	Element	Chemical Form	Common Compounds (Derived from)
Primary	Nitrogen (N)	NO_3^-, NH_4^+	Ammonium nitrate, potassium nitrate
	Phosphorous (P)	$H_2PO_4^-$, HPO_4^{-2}	Potassium phosphate, ammonium phosphate
	Potassium (K)	K^+	Potassium nitrate, potassium chloride
Secondary	Calcium (Ca)	Ca^{+2}	Calcium nitrate, calcium chloride
	Magnesium (Mg)	Mg^{+2}	Magnesium nitrate, magnesium sulfate
	Sulfur (S)	SO_4^{-2}	Zinc sulfate, cobalt sulfate
Micronutrients	Boron (B)	$H_2BO_3^-$	Potassium borate, borax, boric acid
	Chlorine (Cl)	Cl^-	Calcium chloride, potassium chloride
	Cobalt (Co)*	Co^{+2}	Cobalt sulfate, cobalt EDTA
	Copper (Cu)*	Cu^{+2}	Copper sulfate, copper EDTA
	Iron (Fe)*	Fe^{+2}	Iron sulfate, ferrous sulfate, iron EDTA, iron DTPA
	Manganese (Mn)*	Mn^{+2}	Manganese EDTA, manganese sulfate
	Molybdenum (Mo)	MoO_4^{-2}	Ammonium molybdate, sodium molybdate
	Zinc (Zn)*	Zn^{+2}	Zinc EDTA, zinc sulfate

* May come in a chelated form

Table: Primary, Secondary, and Micronutrients and Their Common Chemical Forms

Primary Nutrients (N, P, K)

Nitrogen, phosphorus, and potassium, commonly referred to as "N-P-K" or the "big three," are the primary nutrients for plants. They are considered the "meat and potatoes" of plant nutrition—elements that are heavily used by plants at every stage of their life cycle.

Nitrogen (N)

Nitrogen is available to plants in two forms; ammoniacal nitrogen (NH^+) and nitrate nitrogen (NO_3^-) with nitrate nitrogen being the preferred form for indoor gardening. Nitrogen is the most abundant element we feed to our plants. Carbon, hydrogen, and oxygen are found in higher quantities in plant tissue, but they are derived by the plant from carbon dioxide and water, not fed to the plant by gardeners. Nitrogen is the basis for many of the plant's complex compounds such as chlorophyll, amino acids, proteins, ATP, and even DNA. Without nitrogen, plant life could not happen.

> **Expert Corner**
>
> *Don't believe the heavily promoted myth that flowering plants need less nitrogen during the flowering phase. Many of them need more nitrogen in flower, not less.*

In nature there are two ways a plant can obtain nitrogen. The first is by fixing atmospheric nitrogen (N_2) though the use of an Azotobacter. Azotobacters are bacteria that convert the nitrogen in the air into ammonium ions (NH_4^+) that can be directly fed to the plant or passed to the soil for further processing. The second way is through a process called ammonification. This is where dead plants and animals are broken down (decay) into ammonium, which is also either taken up by the plant or passed into the soil for further processing.

So what's this further processing? It's a process called nitrification that converts ammonium ions (NH_4^+) into nitrate (NO_3^-) through two different forms of bacteria: Nitrosomonas and Nitrobacters.

$$NH_4^+ + \text{Nitrosomonas} \rightarrow NO_2^- + \text{Nitrobacter} \rightarrow NO_3^-$$

One of the ways indoor gardens are different than those found in nature is that we feed indoor gardens from bottles and don't rely on decaying plants and microorganisms to feed the plants. All the

😄 Nitrogen Fun Fact

NH_4^+ *(ammonium) form of N lowers soil pH*
NO_3^- *(nitrate) form of N raises soil pH*

nutritional elements we feed to the plants have to be "readily available," meaning that they are in a form that is easy for the plant to take in and use.

There are several different forms of nitrogen, with varying levels of availability. Complicating matters, nitrogen is also labeled in many different ways. Here are two examples of how nitrogen shows up on nutrient bottle labels:

Total nitrogen	5%
Ammoniacal nitrogen	1%
Water insoluble nitrogen	2%
Water soluble nitrogen	2%

Total nitrogen	2%
Nitrate nitrogen	1.5%
Urea nitrogen	0.3%
Ammoniacal nitrogen	0.2%

- Ammoniacal nitrogen can be directly used by plants. It's critical that you understand that plants can't regulate the uptake of the ammoniacal form of nitrogen; if it's present, they will absorb it. If the plant is not capable of creating and transporting enough sugars to the roots to process this excess nitrogen, ammoniacal nitrogen can overwhelm the plant, causing harm. Be careful when using fertilizers high in ammoniacal nitrogen, especially in hydroponic media. The effect is nullified somewhat in soil/soilless media, as the positively charged ammonia ion will bond with the negatively charged soil particles.
- Water-insoluble nitrogen is a slow-release form of nitrogen. It must be broken down by microorganisms in the grow media before it can be used by the plants.

- Water-soluble nitrogen is just as it sounds—it's all the soluble and readily available forms of nitrogen lumped together. These can include (and not be specifically labeled as) ammoniacal, nitrate, and soluble and readily available forms of nitrogen and urea.
- Nitrate nitrogen can be directly used by plants and is the preferred form for indoor use.
- Stay away from urea in indoor gardening. Urea needs to be converted to a usable form by an enzyme called urease, which is not typically found in indoor grow media.

Phosphorus (P)

Phosphorus is essential for plant life as it's a component of DNA, chlorophyll, phospholipids, nucleotides, and coenzymes—a lot of the stuff that makes plants work. It's involved in stimulating root development, increasing stems and stalk strength, improving flower formation, and increasing resistance to plant diseases. Phosphorus is another one of the three primary or macro nutrients.

Like nitrogen, phosphorus has different forms. Generally in indoor gardening we use phosphorous in the phosphate (Pi) form, which is derived from phosphor<u>ic</u> acid. Another form called phosphite (Phi) is derived from phosphor<u>ous</u> acid. For indoor gardening, phosphite has very limited use. It's used by big agriculture as a fungicide and not as a source of phosphorus. Stay away from products that contain phosphite when growing indoors. You can identify them by looking for "derived from phosphor<u>ous</u> acid" on the label.

If the effects of phosphorus on plants were discovered in more modern times, or at least after analytical chemistry techniques were available, it most likely would not be considered one of the macro elements. It remains considered one of the "big three" more due to when its effects were discovered than the amount used by plants. Tissue analysis and soil sampling has determined that plants use significantly more nitrogen and potassium than phosphorus. This ratio holds true for most plants with both vegetative and flowering states.

Too much phosphorus can kill beneficial microorganisms such as mycorrhizae. Additionally, excessive phosphorus can cause copper, iron, manganese, and zinc deficiencies. Typically, plants require phosphorus at a rate similar to their requirements of calcium or magnesium.

A big trend in indoor gardening is to use "bloom boosters" during a plant's flowering cycle that are heavy in phosphorus and potassium. Bloom boosters come in an array of products that contain little to no nitrogen, extremely large amounts of phosphorus, and quite a bit of potassium. To identify them, look for N-P-K labeling such as "0-50-30". High levels of potassium are great for flowering plants, but plants don't require nearly the amount of phosphorus contained in the typical bloom booster and can be burned by the excess. They should be used only by experienced gardeners.

Phosphorus is labeled as P_2O_5 by law, but that's a bit misleading. See the Commercial versus Elemental Analysis at the end of the chapter for details.

Potassium (K)

Potassium's role in plants is a bit different than the role of other nutrients. It's not actually part of any plant structures, but it assists with most of the functions within a plant. Potassium, also referred to as potash, is often called the "quality nutrient" because of its positive effects of fruiting size, shape, color, taste, and other quality measurements. Some of the other effects of potassium are:

- Increases enzyme production and activation.
- Helps relocation of plant sugars and starches.

- Regulates of stomata for water retention.
- Accelerates root growth.
- Aids with photosynthesis and protein synthesis.
- Improves drought tolerance.
- Helps defend against crop diseases.
- Assists in ion balance control.

Potassium is labeled as K_2O as required by law, but that's a bit misleading. See the Commercial Analysis versus Elemental Analysis section for more information on potassium concentrations.

Secondary Nutrients (Ca, Mg, S)

Calcium, magnesium, and sulfur are classified as secondary nutrients. They are called this because they are consumed in smaller amounts than the primary nutrients but in greater amounts than the seven micronutrients. Secondary nutrients play critical roles and are just as important as NPK.

Calcium (Ca)

Plants, just like humans, need calcium. In humans, calcium builds strong teeth and bones. Similarly, in plants, calcium strengthens cell walls and allows them to bind together. It's a critical element in overall plant growth and has been identified as a factor in increasing nitrogen uptake. Other benefits of calcium are:

- Major component in photosynthesis, critical in the light-dependent reactions that split water molecules.
- Essential for good growth and strong cell wall structure: it forms calcium pectate, which give stability to cell walls and bind cells together.

- Disease prevention—strong cell walls can ward off attack by fungus and bacteria.
- Stimulation of the protein channels that take up nutrients.
- Stomata regulation/heat stress.
- Aids in plant signaling and intracellular regulator.
- Improves fruit quality.

Magnesium (Mg)

Magnesium is critical for plants. It is found in every cell type in all living things—plants, animals, bacteria, and fungus. In plants it serves as the central molecule in chlorophyll and enables productive sugar synthesis. It's also a catalyst for certain enzyme activity—specifically in converting sucrose into glucose and fructose. Some other functions of magnesium are:

- Transportation of phosphorus in the plant.
- Enzyme activation.
- Starch/sugar translocation.
- Plant oil and fat formation.
- Nutrient uptake control.
- Increased iron utilization.

Sulfur (S)

Interestingly enough, sulfur often gets overlooked as a plant nutrient. The big three, NPK, are at the forefront. Next to be recognized are calcium and magnesium—probably because they're sold together in a bottle. Even silicon is better known to indoor gardeners. Sulfur is almost always thought of as a fungicide but rarely discussed as a nutrient—strange for an element that is used by plants almost as much as phosphorus. Some of the major functions of sulfur are:

- Synthesis of vitamins.
- Synthesis of some amino acids.

- Production of proteins.
- Chlorophyll formation.

Micronutrients

Micronutrients are just what they sound like: nutrients that are used in small amounts in compared to the rest. They're also called trace elements or "micros." Although they are used in small quantities, they are critical. Without them, your garden won't produce well and will eventually die. Unless using very bad grow media or cheap nutrients, deficiencies of micronutrients only occur at extreme (either too high or too low) pH levels.

 **Expert Corner**

Many of the micronutrients found in plant nutrient bottles come in a "chelated" form. Chelated forms enable the element to be available to the plant in a broader pH range and to be more stable within the plant.

Elements in chelated forms can be identified by names that contain suffixes such as EDTA, EDDHA, and DTPA.

Boron (B)

Our current knowledge about boron's role in plants is very limited, though recent studies have helped to unlock its purpose in plant growth. Boron has been linked to several critical plant processes, including cell differentiation, cell wall formation, and carbohydrate (sugar) synthesis. Boron has also been shown to be essential for flowering and pollen production.

Plants use very little boron, and too much is toxic. The effective amount of boron is very small, so be careful when using fertilizers with more than trace amounts of it. Generally, most indoor gardeners don't need to worry about boron toxicities or deficiencies if they are using high-quality plant fertilizers.

Chlorine (Cl)

Chlorine is a bit of a misnomer. While chlorine is the name of the element (and how it's labeled), it's not what plants actually consume. Plants make use of chloride (Cl^-), a different, reduced form of chlorine. Nonetheless, it's labeled as chlorine due to labeling regulations.

Chlorine works in tandem with potassium to control stomata opening and closing, critical for the plant to regulate water and CO_2 levels. It also aids in photosynthesis, specifically in the light-dependent reactions, and is responsible for some of the nutrient transport functions within the plant.

Cobalt (Co)

Very little is known about cobalt's role in higher plants. The only known physiological role of cobalt in plants is its involvement in nitrogen fixing by leguminous plants such as green beans. Cobalt is often regarded as a "non-essential"—more on non-essentials at the end of this chapter. It is interesting that many major nutrient manufacturers include cobalt in their formulations even though its role is not understood.

Copper (Cu)

Copper's largest role in plant nutrition is as a catalyst in photosynthesis and transpiration, and it's a constituent of several enzymes that build amino acids and convert them to proteins. Copper is

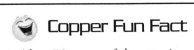

Copper Fun Fact

About 70 percent of the copper in plants is found in chlorophyll.

also important to the formation of lignin in plant cell walls and is known to affect flavor and sugar content.

Iron (Fe)

 **Expert Corner**

Fe^{2+} converts to Fe^{3+} at higher pH ranges. Fe^{3+} is not a readily available form for plants. For this reason, extremely high pH can cause a deficiency in iron.

Iron is essential for the formation of chlorophyll, is a component of cytochromes, is required for nitrogen-fixation processes, and helps to regulate plant transpiration. Like many of the other essential elements used by plants, it has more than one form. Fe^{2+}, also called "ferrous" iron, is the form that's most available to plants at normal pH ranges.

As the pH of the grow media rises, Fe^{2+} can become unavailable to plants. In the real world, iron deficiency is usually not a problem, unless you've managed to get the pH of your root zone completely off base.

Manganese (Mn)

Manganese facilitates the assimilation of CO_2 during photosynthesis, the synthesis of chlorophyll, and the absorption of nitrogen. It also plays a role in the creation of riboflavin and carotenes. Like iron, manganese is unavailable to plants at higher pH levels. Thus, manganese and iron deficiencies often occur together.

Molybdenum (Mo)

Molybdenum (pronounced "mō-LEB-da-num") has a small but important role in plant growth. Its main function is the conversion of nitrates (NO_3^-) into amino acids, which are the building blocks of proteins. Molybdenum is also essential to the conversion of non-available phosphorus into available forms.

Zinc (Zn)

Zinc is highly versatile: it's an essential component of various enzymes, is used in protein synthesis and growth regulation, aids the production of auxin, regulates starch formation, and helps with root development. Additionally, zinc enables plants to withstand lower temperatures.

"Non-Essentials"

In addition to the elements that are directly involved in plant nutrition and function, other nutrients are often found in plant tissues. They are classified as non-essential but still may have noticeable benefits when applied. These include aluminum, sodium, selenium, cobalt, silicon, rubidium, strontium, fluorine, vanadium, and iodine.

Silicon

Silicon is the only non-essential element worth mentioning in detail. Even though it's not directly used by the plant, it is found in very high concentrations within plant tissue—rivaling the levels of nitrogen and potassium. Silicon strengthens cell walls, making the plant less susceptible to insect and fungal attacks. Silicon also improves soil structures, allowing better uptake of micronutrients.

 Silicon Fun Fact

Silicon is found in high concentrations in trichomes, which are small hairs and other structures that grow on the outer surface of a plant. Silicon is responsible for the strength and surface texture of the trichomes.

Most hydroponic nutrients do not generally include silicon in their basic formulas, so you'll have to add it separately to your garden's feeding regimen. For those running "solid" grow media such as rockwool or expanded clay, liquid silicon can be added from a bottle.

Look for the term "potassium silicate" on the label, and you'll know you're using the right stuff.

For those growing in "loose" grow media such as a soil or soilless mix, consider mixing a natural source of silicon into the mix such as diatomaceous earth (DE). DE is comprised of ancient fossilized diatoms, which are a class of algae. It's sold under various names, including Diatomite and Hygromite. There are two basic forms of DE: pebble-sized solid rocks, and powder. Both can be blended into almost any loose grow media. The solid form can be a cost saver since it can be reused after a good cleaning.

The powdered version of DE is also used as a pest control. It kills a bunch of garden pests, including white flies, ants, mites, fleas, and leafhoppers. A thin layer of powdered diatomaceous earth applied to the top of the grow media will

 Sloper Says

If growing in expanded clay, consider using a 50:50 ratio of expanded clay and diatomaceous earth rocks—you will love the results.

help stop pest outbreaks, since its glass-shard structure shreds the exoskeleton of any pest that comes in contact with it—killing them fast. It's completely safe for humans and pets: "food grade" DE is sold in health food stores for human consumption as an aid to health, and in pet stores to control fleas both on animals and in their bedding.

Make sure any diatomaceous earth you use comes from freshwater sources, NOT saltwater sources. With high sodium levels, saltwater DE can quickly turn your grow media toxic. The big hardware stores often sell "pool-grade" DE, which is generally the saltwater version of DE. Pool-grade DE has also been subjected to very high temperatures, converting it to the crystalline form that makes a very good water filter but is dangerous to inhale. Make sure any DE you buy for use in the garden is labeled for use as an insecticide or as food grade.

In addition to DE, there are other powdered forms of silicon that can be incorporated into your grow media. These fall into a category called "rock dust." Rock dust is a common by-product of the gravel industry: it's generated when rocks get crushed. While most rock dust comes from limestone, there are other sources, including volcanic and glacial deposits. In addition to silicon, rock dust powders often provide secondary and trace elements. The actual nutrients in a specific batch of rock dust depend on where it was mined. Glacial rock dust, greensand, and Azomite are common names for these types of products.

It's simple to conduct your own experiments to see whether rock dust or diatomaceous earth is effective for your garden or to see which one is best for your garden's needs. Simply add some to one or two plants when growing several of the same species, and leave the rest as the control group. Do everything exactly the same as before, but keep an eye on your experimental plants—you might be pleasantly surprised at the results.

Vitamin B

Vitamin B is probably the most discussed vitamin used in indoor gardening. Many nutrient manufacturers include B1—also known as thiamine—somewhere in their lineup of bottles. Based on laboratory tests conducted in the 1930's, Vitamin B purportedly reduces transplant shock, promotes root development, and aids in plant growth.

Many university researchers, including Robert Cox, horticulture agent at Colorado State University Cooperative Extension and author of the report "Beware of Gardening Myths," have studied B1. Outside of the lab, in tests designed to measure the impact of B1 on whole plants instead of tissue samples, B1 shows no discernible effect on plant growth. Nutrient products containing B1 typically also include minerals and sometimes plant hormones that may cause treated plants to perform better than untreated plants. But the effects in this case are due to the other ingredients, not the B1.

Vitamin C

Plants, like animals, use Vitamin C for a range of metabolic processes. In plants, Vitamin C is found in the chloroplasts—the cells in which photosynthesis occurs. It acts as an antioxidant, protecting the plant from pollutants and free radicals released by various metabolic processes.

Even though most plants and animals (except humans) produce sufficient supplies of Vitamin C internally to support growth, studies have shown that supplemental Vitamin C increases growth. In 1935, Synnöve and Hausen published a study showing that 40 mg of Vitamin C added to a sterile liquid growing medium increased the dry weight of the treated plants over control plants by 35–75%.

Vitamin D

Just as humans, plants can synthesize their own Vitamin D. Vitamin D has been associated with adventitious root growth (roots forming in new places) as well as calcium transport. In a 1979 paper, Buchala and Schmid suggested that Vitamin D should be part of a new class of plant growth stimulators because of its effectiveness. Currently, there are no nutrients that list Vitamin D as an ingredient, though due to labeling requirements, it might be in the bottle but not disclosed as an ingredient.

Commercial versus Elemental Analysis

Every bottle or bag of plant fertilizer has three large numbers prominently displayed on the label, such as 10-10-10. These numbers indicate the percentage of the "big three" nutrients included in the fertilizer: 10% nitrogen, 10% phosphorous and 10% potassium. But this is one case where "what you see is not what you get," due to another issue with how fertilizers are labeled.

It turns out that labeling rules require phosphorous and potassium to be listed in their oxidized forms, meaning that the compound that's being tested includes other molecules besides the elemental phosphorous and potassium plants use. The actual levels of usable phosphorus and potassium in any fertilizer are quite a bit lower than the percentage listed on the label.

Let's look at that 10-10-10 fertilizer again. Nitrogen gets its full weight since labeling requirements allow it to be measured in its elemental form. Elemental phosphorus is only 4.36% of total weight and elemental potassium is 8.3%, once the extra molecules plants don't eat are removed from the equation.

Why is this important? You need to understand how the fertilizers you're using are formulated, so you'll be better equipped to deal with nutritional deficiencies and toxicities. You could be accidentally under- or over-feeding your garden if you rely on the percentages listed on plant fertilizer without understanding what they mean. Also, the fact that bio-available phosphorous and potassium in any plant food is quite a bit lower than what's listed on the label helps to explain why few gardeners poison their gardens with bloom boosters, since the products aren't as heavy in phosphorus as they could be!

For the geeks here is a bit of chemistry: to convert the oxides to the elemental concentrations we must first consult a periodic table to obtain the atomic weights. We find that oxygen's atomic weight is 16, phosphorus is 31, and potassium is 39. With that it's just some simple math. Basically divide the weight of the element in question by the total weight of the oxide.

How much elemental phosphorus is contained in P_2O_5?

$$P_2 / P_2O_5$$
$$(P+P) / (P+P+O+O+O+O+O)$$

Then substitute in the weights of each element:

$(31+31) / (31+31+16+16+16+16+16) = .436$ or 43.6% elemental phosphorus

How much elemental potassium is contained in K_2O?

$$K_2 / K_2O$$
$$(K+K) / (K+K+O)$$

Then again substitute the weights of each element:

$(39+39) / (39+39+16) = .83$ or 83% elemental potassium.

11. Pest Prevention

Pest prevention for indoor gardens can be a challenge even for the most experienced gardener, and under LEDs it's even harder because small, telltale signs of an infection can be masked and overlooked under the purplish-pink "glow" of LED grow lights.

Many pests effectively "hide" under LEDs, especially during the initial outbreak—which unfortunately is the best time to treat. When growing under LEDs, it's important that you turn them off at least once every few days—or whenever you suspect a problem—to thoroughly inspect your garden. You can turn your LED lights right back on when you're done, since they don't have to cool down before being turned back on. Use a small fluorescent bulb, such as a two-foot strip light, for this inspection. Get right in there and take a good look at the tops, undersides, stems, and branches of the plants. A quick peek won't be enough.

Sticky Traps

Before you can eradicate pests from your garden, you must first identify them. Sticky traps are a great way to determine whether you're dealing with flying pests and if so, which ones. These traps come in various versions depending on the pests they target. The most common ones for indoor gardening are either yellow or blue: yellow is for whiteflies, aphids, and other flying insects, blue for thrips and leafminers. Most gardeners keep sticky traps near the plants' stems at every stage of plant development to provide continual surveillance for flying pests.

Once you've trapped some pests and know what you're combating, you can develop a strategy to wipe them out. If you've trapped some bugs but don't know what they are, take the trap to a garden center or hydroponic shop so they can help with identification and treatment. Do everyone a favor and place it in a Ziploc bag, so you don't spread the infestation to the entire nursery.

Spraying with the Lights On

Many indoor pest infestations are solved by spraying with a substance that will kill the bugs but not ruin your crop. But should you spray with the lights on or off? A common misconception is that spraying must be done with the lights off because the droplets form "micro magnifying glasses" that intensify the light at a particular point and burn the plant. Anyone who's attempted to burn paper with a magnifying glass knows that the glass needs to be significantly above the paper in order to focus enough light energy on a single point to get it to burn. Simply laying the glass on the paper won't do it. That is a long way of saying spraying with the lights on is fine. If it wasn't, how could plants survive a thunderstorm followed by sunshine?

This myth probably got started after someone used poor-quality or contaminated water when spraying and it caused damaged the plants. It's more likely that a high concentration of salts in the spray caused the dark-spot damage than the light and droplets. Yet this myth persists. Even if you feel uncomfortable spraying with the lights on in an HID garden rest assured you can safely spray with the lights on in a LED garden.

Air Filtration

Many of the pests in our gardens come in from the outside during air exchanges. Small pests, fungi, and bacteria can all make their way into the garden though air vents. When using a powered intake fan, consider using a HEPA filter to eliminate this potential source of pests.

HEPA filters are too restrictive to be used with passive vents. If you experience a pest problem in a small garden with passive intake vents, cover the vents with a nylon stocking or "batting" purchased at a fabric store to help keep the little buggers out.

Ladybugs

Ladybugs, also known as lady beetles and ladybird beetles, are a group of beneficial insects that consume a great number of indoor pests including mites, leafhoppers, scales, mealy bugs, aphids, and other soft-bodied insects. Ladybugs are best employed early in an outbreak. For a major outbreak, spraying and/or setting off a bug bomb might be more effective.

Good news for LED-based growers: ladybugs are LED friendly. Anyone who has made the mistake of releasing ladybugs into a grow space with exposed HID lamps (non-air-cooled hood/not protected by a glass lens) knows that those two don't play nicely together. The ladybugs, attracted by the light and heat, fly straight up into the lights and burn up—what a smell! Worse than burned hair. This is *not a problem* with LEDs. The color of the light is not as attractive to ladybugs, and the lights don't get hot enough to fry them.

Azadirachtin (Neem Oil)

Azadirachtin is an oil that is extracted from neem seeds and is fantastic for controlling garden pests. It's available under many names, including Azamax and Azasol. Some brands add additional pest-fighting ingredients. Azadirachtin should be used as your first line of defense against pests that take up residence in your garden. It acts as an insecticide, miticide, and nematicide, thus killing most common insect pests.

Azadirachtin works with multiple modes of action against pests, including repelling them, interrupting their feeding behavior, and regulating their growth. Spray with it every week as a preventative measure—it's nontoxic and can be used right up to the point of harvest.

Cleanliness is Next to Godliness

During the Grow

Keeping you garden clean during the grow is very important. Clean everything you can, anytime anything looks like it needs cleaning or picking up. Dead leaves provide a haven for pests to hide and multiply. They can also spawn fungus and mold and can clog drains, causing flooding. If anything is spilled, clean it up right away. When the floor of your grow space is clean, you can notice problems such as nutrient leaks before they become major events.

Post-Grow Cleanup Procedures

After you have completed your grow, it's time to clean up. There is no right or wrong way to do this as long as you get the grow space completely clean. This is a critical step that is often skipped or skimped on in order to get the next crop going faster.

Good Practice

After a harvest is a great time to check all the fuses in the garden. Many timers and controllers use fuses. A corroded fuse has been the cause of many garden failures.

Assuming you didn't have pest problems, all you need to do is thoroughly wash everything used in the garden. Use a 10–20% bleach solution to clean all trays, buckets, reservoirs, pumps, hoses, timers, controllers, and pruners as well as the floor, walls, and ceiling before starting your next run. Make sure to rinse everything several times with plain water to completely rinse off the bleach.

If you did have pest problems during your last grow, you'll need a more aggressive cleanup. Start by removing all traces of plants from the garden. The type of infestation will dictate the cleaning needed: if you had fungal attacks, bleach the entire room—walls, floor, ceiling, doors, and fixtures—with full-strength bleach. Make sure you have adequate air flow, or wear a respirator, as bleach fumes are not good for you. Wear rubber gloves, long sleeves, and long pants to protect your skin. For pest invaders such as spider mites, use a bug bomb to make sure everything is dead—including the buggers hiding in the cracks. No matter what method you choose, make sure everything is dead, gone, and cleaned up before starting another crop in that space.

For Indoor Gardens, Cleanliness is Next to Godliness

12. Final Thoughts

Even with everything we've covered so far, there are still a few thoughts to pass along that just didn't seem to fit anywhere else. With these final thoughts in mind, you'll be ready to tackle your first LED garden, or to start improving your garden if you're growing with LEDs already and want to step up your game.

Change, Change, Change

LED grow lights are relatively new. Sure, they've been used in research facilities for years, including in far-flung places like the South Pole and outer space. But as consumer-ready grow lights, they're a recent innovation and are still evolving, fast. Much more research is needed to unlock the many mysteries surrounding the design of the perfect LED grow light. What spectra to use? How to position the emitters for maximum impact? What secondary optics to use? How to bring the cost down from the stratosphere?

No doubt, future LED grow lights will be significantly different than the ones being deployed today. Don't let that deter you from buying one today, however. Now is a great time to begin taking advantage of how LED grow lights can make indoor gardening easier and more productive. As the lights evolve, you'll be evolving your skill in using them. Then, when the "perfect" grow light comes to market, you'll be ready to take full advantage of its strengths and prepared to shore up its weaknesses. In essence, you need to ride the train in order to reach the destination and to know where the stops are along the way.

Be warned, however: buying LED grow lights can be as addictive as building grow boxes. I've personally gone through several of both and am still searching for that perfect one…

"LED Grow Lights Don't Work" [...for them]

If you've hung around a hydroponic shop or online indoor garden forum for any length of time, you've heard this: "LED grow lights don't work." Many self-purported "experts" have had trouble using LEDs and feel the need to tell everyone. It's like they're garden lighting superheroes out to save the growing community from a dire threat. Not even willing to have a conversation, most of these blowhards just bash anyone and everyone who even mentions the three evil words—"LED grow lights."

Don't let somebody else's bad experience limit your options. I've communicated with a lot of these growers, and almost without exception they bought an early or cheap LED grow light (or built their own from cheap components) and have limited-to-zero gardening skills. They try to use an LED grow light exactly the same way they would use an HID light, which from reading this book you know is a recipe for disaster. Their stories mostly go the same: he or she tried growing with an LED light, and based on poor results partway through the grow, switched back to an HID to save their harvest. That's not an experiment. That's just a regrettable grow.

These people will never learn new tricks, because they are unwilling to experiment and *learn* from the results. Change is hard for some people, and that's OK. One size generally does not fit all. LED grow lights are not for everyone.

My advice—just like the old joke of adding "...in bed" when reading a fortune cookie—is to mentally add "...for them" whenever you hear or read someone say that LED grow lights don't work. Simply walk away from these people and think to yourself, "LED grow lights don't work... for them." We all have different goals in our lives as well as our gardens. Blanket statements like "LED grow lights don't work" are just plain silly and expose that person's inability to adapt.

Not Trying to Reproduce Sunlight

One of the things I can't stress enough is that we're trying to grow plants indoors, not reproduce sunlight. Many times grow lights are compared to the sun, with some light manufacturers bragging about how much better their light is because it more accurately reproduces sunlight. After all, the sun is the "big bulb in the sky" under which everything grows, so this makes a good sales pitch.

Don't get caught up in the hype. As we discussed in the photosynthesis section, plants use certain frequencies of light much more than others, and LED grow lights are specifically designed to include only those frequencies most helpful for growing plants. The ONLY thing your garden wants when it comes to light is sufficient quantities of the right spectra to fuel photosynthesis and support plant growth-signaling needs. HID lights emit a *lot* of light in frequencies not needed for these processes, wasting energy and generating excess heat that requires even more wasted energy to remove.

Keep your eye on the ball. Mimicking the sun is not important. Photosynthesis is.

Be a Gardener, Not an Engineer

Keep focused: the point of gardening is to produce big, good-tasting harvests, not to build the most elaborate grow room. Too much of the time, growers focus on their grow room, attempting to precisely control each variable (temp, humidity, CO_2, etc.) until the garden itself becomes an afterthought. These "engineer growers" are not done until there is at least one of every gadget in the grow room. They want to check all of their meters and controllers before making a decision. Don't be this type of gardener.

True gardeners checks their plants regularly and responds to what the plants are telling them. They know what to look for, and if they see a problem, they have an idea about the possible culprit even before glancing at their meters and gauges. It's better for your garden and your wallet for you to develop these skills before you run out and buy more gadgets. You'll probably kill a few plants in the process, but you will learn. Unfortunately, there is no substitute for experience. Be this type of gardener.

Experiment to Completion

Experiments have little value unless taken to a true end point that has meaning. For example, when experimenting with different cloning techniques, you need to take some using your regular method and some with the experimental procedure. Both sets need to be grown to maturity and then the results compared. You can't base your "results" on how fast the cuttings root or how bushy the roots are, or you might be missing something important. These clones need to be grown and harvested to really know if there's a difference. You might be creating a "robbing Peter to pay Paul" situation: something you did to decrease rooting time might cost you later in harvest size or quality. Interim results are helpful for understanding how your change affects the process, but the only result that truly matters is your harvest.

After you've completed your experiment, do it again several times to see whether the result was real or a fluke. When you can consistently produce the same results from the same experiment after multiple tries, your results begin to have merit. Then try it *this* way, and *that* way, and *the other way* too—repeatedly, until you've exhausted every way you can think of and have a large collection of results. Only *then* will you have a dataset that you can begin to draw conclusions from. Experimenting is not a one-time thing. It's a process that takes method, time, repetition, consistency, and patience.

On the subject of experiments, to know anything for sure, you need these experiments to be based in real science—your eyes or taste buds won't replace scientific instrumentation. Multiple "runs" on a chemical analysis machine such as a gas chromatograph–mass spec machine (GC-MS) or atomic absorption instrument are necessary to provide real answers. In order to gather any real information, multiple samples from varying heights, nodes, or branches, not just the top pinnacle fruit from multiple harvests must be averaged to get real data. Unfortunately, this type of advanced lab equipment isn't generally available to ordinary gardeners, though there are a few labs that advertise online and in gardening magazines that will do the analysis for a fee. If you have a friend who works for a research lab, maybe they can help out. Otherwise, experiment all you want, and draw your conclusions. Just don't make the mistake of calling your results "scientific" in front of a real scientist, or you're likely to get laughed out of the room!

Grams per Watt

Every gardener likes to brag about harvest size. The most common way indoor gardeners brag is to quote their yields in terms of weight per watt of electricity consumed. For example, if a grower produced 2.2 pounds/1,000 grams under a 1000-watt HID lamp, the harvest would be described as "one gram per watt."

This is a terrible way to measure garden output. The first problem is that a 1000-watt lamp can consume up to 1,100 watts depending on the ballast, so the "watts" side of the equation is likely off. Secondly, electricity used to power the ventilation systems, air conditioning, nutrient pumps, timers, and controllers doesn't get added into the watt count, so the "watts" are even farther off. These extra watts can really change the "grams per watt" calculation. Unless the entire grow room is on a separate electric meter, it's almost impossible to determine actual the electrical consumption. Anything else is an estimate.

It's OK to use grams per lamp size to tell if your harvest weight went up or down for any given run, but it's no good for bragging rights. Besides, grams per watt focuses on the wrong thing—the weight instead of the quality of your harvest. Let the other growers brag all they want—just show them your harvest. If you've done a good job, your harvest will speak for itself.

Ease per Weight

It's far more valuable, in my opinion, to focus on "ease per weight." Considering ease per weight helps you focus on making changes that make gardening easier on *you*—things you can do, buy, or change to spend less time and effort while maintaining a healthy and bountiful indoor garden. This is one of the driving forces that led me to experiment with LED grow lights: I needed a garden that produced less heat and consumed less electricity, because I spent way too much time stressing about summertime high garden temperatures and inflated utility bills. Along the way I made other changes, such as switching from hydroponics to charged soils so I could primarily feed with water—eliminating clogged feed lines, simplifying spill cleanup, and getting rid of the stinky slime in my reservoir that required odor control during a grow and aggressive reservoir scrubbing after harvest. These changes dramatically simplified my gardening life and over time improved the quality and quantity of my harvests.

Quality per Harvest/Gardening Zen

Which leads us to the most important garden performance metric: "quality per harvest." Who cares if you can grow tons of inedible junk? Indoor gardening is about growing *the largest quantity of the best quality you can for the least expenditure of resources*. After all, you're spending your life energy in your garden. You should reap the benefits of that effort by producing the best that can be grown. Quality per harvest is where bragging rights are properly placed.

Increasing harvest quality while maintaining weight, minimizing watts used, and simplifying the experience should be every indoor gardener's goal. There are thousands and thousands of ways to grow plants indoors. Rarely, if ever, is a particular technique or product critical to the success of a garden. The gardener's skill, and a little luck sometimes, matters much more.

Thus, even though LED grow lights forever changed my gardening life for the better, they might not work for you. It's OK if they don't—though if you follow the advice in this book, they probably will. Constantly scan the horizon for new products or techniques that address the challenges you're experiencing in your garden. *Thoughtfully try new things, find what works for you, make it easy, and make it your own.*

This is gardening Zen. Namaste.

↓ **Cost** ↑ **Yield**
↓ **Labor** ↑ **Quality**
↓ **Energy** ↑ **Harmony**
↓ **Strife** ↑ **Peace**

About the Author

Christopher Sloper has a Bachelors of Science in Chemistry and a MBA. He enjoys gardening and experimenting with cutting edge technology. This is probably what led him to LED grow lights in the first place.